DATED & DATABLE
ENGLISH MANUSCRIPT BORDERS

c. 1395–1499

Cover: *Liber contra duodecim errores & hereses* (Pl. Ia, detail)

feathering, bearing gold balls with round lobes, 1473/4

rounded aroid flower
with folded acanthus, 1448–1455

elongated acanthus leaves,
1499–1500

trefoil with round lobes, 1448–1455

single leaves shaded in self-colour, *c.* 1496

spiky acanthus with (L.) sprig and (R.) spray, 1410–13

Late fourteenth- and fifteenth-century English motifs (not to scale)

DATED & DATABLE ENGLISH MANUSCRIPT BORDERS

c. 1395–1499

KATHLEEN L. SCOTT

THE BIBLIOGRAPHICAL SOCIETY

———

THE BRITISH LIBRARY

To my husband David

'The proof that the little prince existed is that he was charming,
that he laughed, and that he was looking for a sheep.
If anybody wants a sheep, that is a proof that he exists.'

The Little Prince, by A. de Saint-Exupéry

© The Bibliographical Society 2002

First published in 2002 by the Bibliographical Society
and The British Library
96 Euston Road, London NW1 2DB

ISBN 0 948170 12 3 (Bibliographical Society)
0 7123 4742 9 (British Library)

A CIP Catalogue record for this book is
available from The British Library

22107SSX

Printed and bound in Great Britain by
Henry Ling Limited, at the Dorset Press,
Dorchester, DT1 1HD

Designed by David Chambers

SHORT LIST OF DATED & DATABLE ENGLISH MANUSCRIPT BORDERS *c.* 1395–1499

Pl. I: Cambridge, Trinity Hall, MS 17, Roger Dymok, *Liber contra duodecim errores & hereses Lollardorum.* *c.* 1395–Sept. 1399.

Pl. II: Oxford, Bodleian Library, MS Bodley 316, Ranulf Higden, *Polychronicon*; etc. *c.* 1394–1397.

Pl. III: London, British Library, Harley MS 401, *Floretum evangelicum.* 1396.

Pl. IV: Eton, College Library, MS 108, [2 MSS] ff. 1r–110v, Augustine, *De Trinitate* (XIV); ff. 112r–185v, William Norton, *Tabula super doctorem de Lyra*; etc. *c.* 1403.

Pl. V: London, British Library, Harley MS 2946, Breviary. 1405.

Pl. VI: Oxford, Bodleian Library, MS Laud Lat. 4, ff. 1r–147r John of Salisbury, *Polycraticus.* 1406.

Pl. VII: Oxford, Bodleian Library, MS Fairfax 2, Wycliffite Bible. 1408.

Pl. VIII: London, British Library, Arundel MS 38, Thomas Hoccleve, *Regiment of Princes.* 1410–1413.

Pl. IX: Chelmsford, Essex Record Office D/B 3/13/7, Inspeximus and confirmation charter of 31 Edward III. 1416.

Pl. X: London, British Library, Harley Charters 51.H.6, Inspeximus concerning Lincolnshire. 1421/2.

Pl. XI: Cambridge, University Library, MS Gg.4.19, Philip de Monte Calerio, *Postilla super evangelia dominicalia*, Pt. II. 1425.

Pl. XII: Glasgow, University Library, MS Hunter 215 (U.2.6), *Cartularium prioratus Sanctae Trinitatis infra Aldgate.* 1425–1427.

Pl. XIII: Cambridge University Library, MS Ff.3.27, ff. 1r–45r, John Sharpe, *Abbreviacio quodlibetorum Duns Scoti.* 1429.

Pl. XIV: Oxford, Bodleian Library, MS Bodley 795, William Holme, *De simplicibus medicinis*; etc. 1435.

Pl. XV: London, British Library, Royal MS 5.F.ii, ff. 1r–31v Athanasius, *De humanitate verbi contra gentes*; etc. 1439 – before 1443/4.

Pl. XVI: Oxford, Balliol College, MS 28, Thomas Docking, *Super Deuteronomium.* 1442.

Pl. XVII: Oxford, Bodleian Library, MS Duke Humfrey b.1, John Capgrave, *Commentarius in Exodum.* 1440 – before Feb. 1444.

Pl. XVIII: London, Public Record Office, E 164/10. *Nova statuta Angliae. c.* 1445/6.

Pl. XIX: Oxford, Bodleian Library, MS Bodley 362, ff. 1r–247v, John of Gaddesden, *Rosa medicinae*; etc. 1448–1455.

Pl. XX: Cambridge, University Library, MS Ee.5.21, ff. 29r–127r, *Registrum statutorum ecclesie et consuetudinum cathedralis sancti Pauli londoniarum*; etc. 1450.

Pl. XXI: Oxford, Bodleian Library, MS Bodley 361, Medical miscellany, incl. pp. 1–111, Stephen Arnald, *Dietarium*; etc. 1453, 1455, 1456, 1459.

Pl. XXII: Winchester, College Library, MS 13B, Genealogical Chronicle. *c.* 1453.

Pl. XXIII: Oxford, Exeter College, MS 62, Hugh of St. Cher, *In Matthaeum et Marcum*. 1454.

Pl. XXIV: Oxford, Bodleian Library, MS Lat. theol. b.5, pp. 1–524, Hugh of St Cher, Commentary on Isaiah; etc. 1456; 1455.

Pl. XXV: London, Lambeth Palace, MS 15, 42-line Bible, New Testament (printed book). *c.* 1455.

Pl. XXVI: Oxford, Balliol College, MS 204, John Duns Scotus, *Ordinatio IV*. 1461.

Pl. XXVII: Oxford, Bodleian Library, MS 108 John Bury, *Gladius Salomonis*. *c.* 1457–*c.* 1461.

Pl. XXVIII: Oxford, Bodleian Library, MS e Musaeo 42, Genealogical Chronicle. 1467–1469.

Pl. XXIX: London, St Paul's Cathedral, Archive of the College of Minor Canons, deposited Guildhall Library, London, as MS 29413, Letters Patent of Edward IV. 1468.

Pl. XXX: London, Guildhall Library, MS 8695, Charter of Incorporation of the Pewterers' Company. 1473/4.

Pl. XXXI: Glasgow, University Library, MS Hunter 77 (T.3.15), Nicholas Love, *Mirror of the Blessed Life of Jesus Christ*. 1474/5.

Pl. XXXII: Luton, Art Museum, Luton Guild Register. 1475.

Pl. XXXIII: London, Skinners' Company, Book of the Fraternity of the Assumption of Our Lady. 1477/8.

Pl. XXXIV: London, belonging to the Wax Chandlers' Company, Charter of Incorporation to Company of the Wax Chandlers. 1484.

Pl. XXXV: London, British Library, Additional MS 33736, Pietro Carmeliano, *Suasoria laetitiae ad Angliam pro sublatis bellis civilibus. . . epistola*. *c.* 1486.

Pl. XXXVI: London, Victoria and Albert Museum, National Library of Art, MS L. 4362-1948, Grant of Arms by John Wrythe to Hugh Vaughn. 1492.

Pl. XXXVII: London, Public Record Office, E 164/11, *Statuta Angliae*. *c.* 1496.

Pl. XXXVIII: Oxford, Merton College, MS 23, St Jerome, *In duodecim minores prophetas*. 1497.

Pl. XXXIX: Oxford, Bodleian Library, MS Selden supra 77, William Parron, *De astrorum vi fatali*. 1499–1500.

INTRODUCTION

Apart from illustrations, borders are the most important – and most frequent – major element of decoration in late fourteenth- and fifteenth-century English manuscripts.[1] Yet borders have received little chronological or systematic study, that is, no analysis of their structure and components within a given period[2] and no scrutiny that would record aspects of change in border elements and identify the chronology of design in structure and motif. A leaf drawn and coloured in one period does not fold or reflect light as in a later period, and its colour tonality may be rendered by different methods. Since borders seem to alter in style at a quicker chronological pace than the work of scribes, borders provide a narrower dating for a manuscript. Researchers who might otherwise have 'dated' their copy of a text to 'the fifteenth century' might be able, with some visual command of the development of English borders, to apply a period of at least a quarter-century to a book, a more acceptable range for discussion and study. At the same time, a systematic analysis of dated and datable borders would furnish terminology for description of other borders in other contexts.

A further significant reason to survey later English borderwork is for an understanding of the hierarchical use of borders. Borders were employed to suggest the structure of a text, and it is helpful to know that a band or trellis border is a sign of the introductory page of a text (cf. Pl. II), even if followed by further band borders at book (rather than chapter) divisions; to know that a three-sided border is of lesser status than a full border; that, unless it occurs at a Table of Contents (cf. Pl. xxxia–b), the first border in a book is usually more elaborate, even if only by a few motifs, than the subsequent borders (cf. Pl. xxia–b); or to know that the most important border, identifiable by its position (usually the first text page) and its more elaborate rendering, may be by an artist different from the rest of the borders and initials in the book, a common hierarchy of style and/or ability (cf. Pl. xxxviiia–b). A sense of the hierarchy of borders has implications for understanding the medieval response to a given text and for the reconstruction of disarranged books.

A presentation of a century of English borders, even if limited to fewer than forty manuscripts, also enables an assessment of English book art in the period. What is the quality in a given decade? Do styles overlap? What are the implicit aesthetic criteria at each period or overall? How quickly does change in border style come? What structures and what motifs are constants throughout the period c. 1395 to c. 1499? Which drop from the stock? Is there notable foreign influence? If so, when does it occur, and on what aspect of English design does it have an impact? The history of English borderwork and of foreign influence on it cannot be assumed to accompany, as a sort of substratum, the meanderings or outcrops of foreign illustration in English manuscripts: outside influences may have affected borders at different times and from different sources than those affecting miniatures. The range of styles, cultural identity, adeptness of assimilation, excellence or lack of it in terms of implicit English standards, and answers to the questions just raised become evident through a chronological series of borders. Furthermore, apart from a few exceptions (e.g. Pls xva–b, xxvi, xxxviiia, xxxix), many of the designs and motifs in this handbook are so English in style that they should not be mistaken for anything but English work, and this kind of recognition should be one of the more important outcomes of the survey, even if the diversity of renderings within the English style is truly remarkable (cf. e.g. Pls xviii, xix).

Before surveying the development of the fifty borders and spray initials reproduced here,[3] I want first to define the scope of the decorative work included, reserving a discussion of the serious problems inherent in a survey of dated and datable borders for concluding remarks. It is essential to say at once that no border of the period of this handbook survives securely dated by the limner.[4] The date of the borders given here derives from inscriptions by the scribes, and the borders are assumed to have been entered more or less concurrently with the copying of the text (especially in books with only one or two borders) or shortly afterwards, i.e. within a year (a reasonable allowance of time for the majority of illuminated manuscripts).[5] It is rare to find illuminated borders looking seriously at odds with this assumption, though occasional blanks or ruled spaces for borders raise the possibility that some borders were done later. The term 'datable' is here defined as within a six-year span (cf. Pl. xxia–b) in order to limit the possiblity of change in decorative styles within the datable period. The only manuscript allowed any lee-way in dating is MS Bodley 108 (Pl. xxviia–b), which can be 'dated' after the time of composition in 1457 and c. 1461, when a number of other manuscripts were decorated by the same hand in East Anglia. This hand and style are of such consequence that the manuscript was included.

Only borders made in pigments and gold were included here, and flourishwork borders, i.e. borders made of penwork, usually in red, blue and/or purple ink or wash, and rarely with gold (cf. Pl. 1b, col. B), were excluded.[6] Printed books with hand-made borders in pigments and gold were taken account of, if only one such border could, for various reasons, be included (Pl. xxv). A few dated manuscripts with borders possibly or probably by a non-English artist have been admitted to the selection, either because of their influence on English shops (Pl. xxvi) or because of their apparent collaboration with an English limner (Pl. xxxviiia–b); certain other borders here (Pls xxxvb, xxxviib, xxxix) may appear to be by a foreign craftsman but are more likely to be by an English artist imitating a foreign style. There is no discussion of the stages involved in the making of a border or in the preparation of materials used in their making.

Probably the most fundamental change that occurs in English borderwork and that is demonstrated in the handbook is a movement from rigid, straight, and attached motifs and designs to curling, circular, and disassociated designs. Bar-frames that are by nature rigid and in 'control' of the text space disappear in favour of curling sprays used as a border frame. The sprays and their feathering also evolve from straight (or just off straight: Pls Ib, IIIb) to a curl at the end (Pls VII, bottom; VIII, bottom) or to a curl and split (Pl. vb, bottom), to a waving form (Pl. va, vb, R. side), and finally to waving feathering with a branch looped back to form a circular shape (Pls X, XX). The evolution from straight to curving forms may be evident in the same manuscript on the same border (Pl. VIII) or chronologically in overlapping spurts (Pls X, XI), but it is nevertheless a distinct evolution or change of taste towards curvilinear forms. While the larger designs are changing in a curvilinear direction, small pointed motifs are also becoming more rounded or curved and/or curled back on themselves, as well as presented in profile. The profile view may even have come about in order to accentuate the rounded outline of this new mode. These folded or turned-back leaf forms, together with a softer means of shading in self-colour (other than by lines and dots), also encouraged a contrast of dark and light and a resulting sense of modelling and illusionistic depth to motifs (cf. Pl. IX, initial infilling and leaf motifs in sprays). The earlier rows of leaf motifs (cf. Pls Ia, L., va, above initial, VII) become less regimented, develop into larger less formalized postures, and seem to flap and wave about from corners and midpoints of the bar (Pls XVI, XVIIa, XX), even though still connected to a vine or bar source.

In the fourth quarter of the century, in some cases under the influence of continental border designs, the sprays become disconnected from the bars to emerge with less rationale directly from initial corners (Pls XXVIII, XXX, XXXIb, XXXIII), or, with less or no feathering, as branches largely independent of each other and of the structure given by the still present bar-frame and cornerpieces (Pl. XXXII). The bar-frame may also disappear completely in favour of unconnected sprays, feathering, branches, and motifs (Pls XXXIV–vb), while in a few borders the feathering may still act as structure and support for motifs (Pl. XXXVI). The final stage shows a complete disappearance of spraywork and feathering and a separation of motifs from each other, with the decoration contained only by a rose pen frame and wash gold ground (Pl. XXXIX). The sense of a sequence of motifs originating from spraywork with a vine and/or pen feathering is lost, and the motifs are enlarged beyond functioning as smaller motifs hanging on a vine to the size of individual set-pieces. The traditional English border had at least one notable virtue: a metaphorical, as it were, connection with the text, which it enhanced, not competed with, in that it developed from the first letter of the text. The severing of this connection not only produced a loss of coherence in design but required a new kind of decorative frame (the rose pen frame) for motifs that needed to be viewed as a presence in themselves rather than as part of a hierarchical adjunct to the text.[7] The conventional fifteenth-century English border was not understandable without each previous part of the border, that is, the spray was understood as developing (admittedly, fantastically) from a leaf or (aroid) flower or row of leaves which in turn grew from a vine at the end of the bar-frame or a vine which had developed from the first letter of the text (Pls XIX, XXIIIa). The English border was, while having on the whole fewer naturalistic motifs than continental borders, at least somewhat natural or organic in over-all structure (cf. Pl. xxvIII with Pl. xxxIV). The continental border was usually 'connected' by myriad small motifs and pen squiggles and short vines entered as a dense background behind the larger painted motifs (Pl. xxxIV). This evolution in border design reached a manner of logical conclusion when the background was omitted entirely, leaving only the major naturalistic motifs without support or context (Pl. xxxIX).

The bar-frame border has a long history as a text-framing device in English manuscripts. But before this type of border came to be used as a frame, the growth of a vine extension from the corner or tail of an initial had to be set in motion. This concept happened in the thirteenth century, possibly *c.* 1220. The vine extensions soon developed leaves, and then grew by the mid-thirteenth century to lengths recognizable as bar borders and/or widened to resemble band borders. A true three-sided border[8] can be found by *c.* 1280–90, but thereafter both full and partial borders remained unsettled in design and structure, often canting away from the text space, incorporating grotesques (Pl. II) or vines as part of the bar structure, or forming a border from unattached segments of decoration. The full and three-sided bar border began to subside into a single basic design in the late fourteenth century (Pl. Ia–b), if sometimes continuing into the fifteenth century to use vines to complete a four-sided border (Pl. vb). When in the last period the full border became relatively fixed, as early as *c.* 1405 (Pls IV, va), it did not change its basic form until either being replaced by an unstructured continental design in the later fifteenth century or until ceasing to be used entirely in the sixteenth.

The three-sided border was somewhat more variable than the full bar border in the period *c.* 1395–1499. Three-sided borders in the late thirteenth and fourteenth centuries had bars or vines, sometimes on a gold background, that ended in a short vine-sprouting of usually three or so leaves,[9] and these frames also usually had some kind of decorative elaboration at the corners, often, as in the fifteenth century, a roundel or massing of leaves. With time, the brief sprays grew, as it were, backwards, causing first the upper and lower bars to retreat, and then later the vine supporting the motifs. These early short sprays of vines bore only coloured motifs (for similar sprays, see the R. border of Pl. II); after its appearance perhaps *c.* 1350, the gold ball was by *c.* 1370–80 combined in the sprays with coloured leaves, thereby setting a design that was to be used as long as English borders were made in the Gothic style. The Litlyngton Missal of 1383–84 (Westminster Abbey MS 37) is unusual in having sprays of only gold balls on a pen vine, a theme never as popular as the mixed-motif spray; but the gold-ball spray was used later from time to time in a lengthened version (cf. Pl. xxx). The next evolution in England of these sprays was the application of each type separately to a different type of initial: the 'champ' initial became largely identified with a spray of feathering and gold motifs only, whereas the spray or 'sprynget' initial normally had a spray of both coloured and gold motifs.[10]

Sprays in three-sided borders were in the late fourteenth and early fifteenth centuries normally composed of a coloured, usually green, vine that held motifs on two sides (Pls ib, iiib); the vines tended to be straight or slightly wavy rather than curling until as late as 1429 (e.g. Pl. xiii); and only short pen lines that had probably been introduced in the 1380s were used between the motifs without leaf lobes/finials. By 1408 (Pls vii, viii) the stiff coloured vine was in retreat back to the gold ground, afterwards occurring sporatically, but in the main giving way to curvilinear feathering as the support for motifs and as adjuncts to the bar-frame, whether full (Pl. xviii) or partial (Pl. xx). Raceme-like feathering was not a feature of thirteenth and fourteenth century borders and its presence should identify a manuscript, at least broadly, as fifteenth century. From about 1405 (Pl. vb, lower spray), the feathering of sprays began to form a distinct curl, a phenomenon in the lower, wider border first, while the upper spray remained straight (Pls vii, viii, xviib) or somewhat straighter (Pl. xx). By about 1450 usually both the upper and lower sprays fell into rolling waves, sometimes with a very dense display of feathering and motifs (Pl. xxia).

The final kind of border to be mentioned here[11] is the spray border, which is composed of a large initial and of spraywork across most or all of a margin. These appear from early in the century, here 1416 (Pl. ix) until quite late, here 1492 (Pl. xxxvi) and may be English (Pls xxiv, xxviii, xxxia) or continental (Pl. xxvi) in style, with initials of either coloured letters on a gold ground or gold on a coloured ground, in one (Pl. xxix), two (Pl. xxviii), or more margins (Pl. xxxia). They seem to have had no special function, as they occur on first-text pages and at the head of documents; but they may have been less costly than a partial bar-frame.

As with border types, it is not possible to trace and discuss all motifs known at this period. Only those with a beginning or end-date, even if approximate, will be mentioned, or those with a considerable life-span but with a change in style or rendering. Among the earlier motifs that are indicative of date is a pattern of gold filler-motifs set, like a spike, between coloured leaves that occur in rows or in groups on a gold background. This gold motif (Pls ia–b, va–b) appears until about 1405, at which time the points become rounded and less extreme and the rows of leaves begin to disappear from the border design. Another early indicator motif is the curled leaf in colour that was apparently introduced in the Trinity Hall MS (Pl. ib, lower spray). Whereas throughout the fourteenth century leaves of all sorts had been depicted as flat on the page and shown from a top or frontal view, this leaf is rolled up with illusionistic depth and seen from the side. It continues in use until at least c. 1435 (Pl. xiv). Another very early illusionistic treatment of motifs involves the use of vines, which may twist over and under each other, especially in interlaces (Pls ii, iv), or disappear under a gold ground to emerge from below it (Pls ia–b). Interlaces are used rarely after 1410, and, if so, probably as a deliberate archaizing feature (e.g. Tokyo, Takamiya MS 24, Devonshire Chaucer, c. 1470, ff. 1r, 53v). The disappearing vine trick is performed occasionally later in the century (cf. Pl. xi, upper border). Daisy buds are another fourteenth-century motif, at least as old as the 1320s, that last through that century (Pl. IIIa) into the turn of the fifteenth and then become rare. The kidney, heart, and kite leaves, the trumpet, and the barbed quatre- and cinquefoil came into use in the fourteenth century and continued, according to the artist, in the fifteenth.

Most of the leaf forms used in the fourteenth century were of four kinds: maple-like (Pl. II, lower border), oak, holly (Pl. Ia, upper R. spray), and trefoils with either pointed (possibly meant to be ivy) or distinctly rounded lobes (Pl. XIII, upper border); nondescript leaf shapes can of course also be found. The maple-leaf design did not last much past 1400; the rounded trefoil is seldom known past 1400, apart from a few Salisbury borders (Pl. XIX); and the holly shows up off and on in the fifteenth century (Pl. VIII, upper spray) but is not a preferred motif. More amorphous, vaguely shaded, two- and three-lobed leaves (Pl. va–b) were used throughout the fifteenth century (cf. Pls XX, XXV, XXXIa, XXXVIIa).

Acanthus is, as Valentine says,[12] 'perhaps the most widely used leaf form in manuscripts ornament' and is therefore of less use in approximate dating of borders. One form in English books has, however, a relatively abrupt starting point and a chronologically short use. The coloured, deeply folded and/or twisted acanthus with spiky lobes that appears at the top and bottom of the bar in MS Arundel 38 (Pl. VIII) of 1410–13 is quite distinctive from traditional forms of the leaf (Pl. II, infilling of band border; Pl. X, initial stems). The curled/folded spiky acanthus outlined in black is found normally no later than c. 1430, the latest example reproduced here being of 1425–27 (Pl. XII, corners). Aroids, another important motif in the century, do not come in until c. 1420–25 (Pl. X), possibly from a French source, but become rampant by the later 1430s and 1440s, especially in Oxford shops (Pl. XIV). Later they are much enlarged and used with layers of curled leaves in initials (Pl. XVIII), at corners (Pl. XIX), at mid-points of bars (Pl. XVIII, lower), and at tops and bottoms of bars (Pls XXIa, XXIIIa), apparently throughout England.

Although gold balls with a pen-and-ink squiggle and/or with short, straight lines are found in English borders as early as the 1330s,[13] they do not acquire a green tint until the fifteenth century, probably sometime between c. 1408 and c. 1413 (Pl. VIII); unfortunately this does not mean that every border after c. 1413 was coloured with green tint on these gold motifs (Pl. IX). Another gold design, the pine cone with prickly black finishing strokes, seems to have come into fashion around 1435 (Pl. XVIII; and London, Drapers' Co., Grant of Arms, 1439) and was in borders until the end of the century (Pl. XXXVIIIb), and occasionally in the early 16th century.

Shading on coloured motifs, usually leaves, continues, as applied in the fourteenth century, in the form of bands of white, circles of white, and white shading along the edges of leaves (all on Pl. II, lower border; Pl. IV), or as lines of white dots (Pl. II), outlining in white, or a series of parallel strokes in white (Pl. II, R. border). By c. 1405 (Pl. vb), white shading along the vertical axis on half of a leaf had come in, giving the leaf a two-toned, more modelled effect in self-colour, especially as the leaves had at the same time assumed a more curved or animated form. As we see in Pls VI, VII, VIII, and XIII, this change was not instantaneous and probably not widespread until about c. 1425, the various types of shading on coloured pigment co-existing for sometime in the same borders (Pl. XIII).

The introduction of naturalistic flora, apart from the leaf types mentioned above in the fourteenth century, is sporadic in the extreme in the fifteenth century, with the representation of animals, birds, and human figures apparently taking precedence. Realistically depicted columbines were used in the late fourteenth century (Pl. II), and much earlier c. 1310–20;[14] the magnificent Sherborne Missal[15] (BL Add. MS 74236) of 1396–1407 used sprays of recognizable flowers and vines; and realistic sprigs were employed as an owner's designation in Brussels, Bibliothèque Royale, MS IV.1095, c. 1415–20,[16] as were roses as badges in borders throughout the century and earlier. Other flora appeared sporadically in borders (e.g. Cambridge, Gonville and Caius MS 247/473, f. 1r, strawberries) until in San Marino, Huntington Library HM 268,[17] after 1438/9–c. 1440–50, naturally rendered plants, fruits, and flowers became a major presence as sprays in partial borders. The mode does not become permanent and widely exploited in full bar borders until introduced from continental sources around 1450–60 (cf. Pl. XXVI), if often together with an English structure (Pl. XXXII) or motifs (Pls XXXIV–V). Large branches of roses, carnations, thistles, and strawberries may have been introduced into England by the Caesar Master between 1448 and c. 1460; but his first manuscript with an extensive array of these naturalistic flora (BL Add. MS 62523) can unfortunately not be dated any more closely than c. 1450.[18] Other manuscripts[19] might also have introduced the branch motifs but all are only datable between c. 1450 and c. 1465, leaving Balliol College MS 204 (Pl. XXVI) of 1461 as the first dated example.

Around 1400 the use of grotesques (as in Pl. II, upper R. corner) and of other animate if unlikely figures disappears from English borders, apart from borders under intense foreign influence (Pls XVa–b). When inhabited borders re-appear twenty to twenty-five years later in such manuscripts as BL Add. 42131, Bedford Hours and Psalter, c. 1420, and as Add. 50001, Hours of Elizabeth the Queen, 1420–1430, they are often enclosed within roundels at corners or in trelliswork (cf. Pl. XXII, of a later date). They do not become a true presence again until between 1450–60 (Pls XXII, XXXII, XXXIV).[20] Nevertheless, it is noteworthy how many English borders after this decade do *not* contain grotesques or other animate (non-floral) motifs.

This handbook of borders has inherent complications, some of which can be fore-seen and described, and it has the potential to mislead users unless the pitfalls of working with dated and datable borders are kept in mind. The possibility that a border may have been entered considerably later than the date of writing has already been mentioned; no such border has knowingly been included here. Where a place of writing is mentioned by the scribe, it is of course also clearly possible that the book was decorated in a different locale; excepted from this general statement would be documents written in London/Westminster and books such as MS Bodley 108 (Pls xxviia–b), where the style is known from other sources to be indicative of the locale.

Another possible difficulty relating to this handbook concerns the selection of manuscripts. Those included had to be chosen from a reasonably large group of surviving dated or datable manuscripts, about 200 to date, and this is not to speak of hand-made borders in documents and printed books. The problem here was how best to select among these. Was it better to concentrate on London/Westminster as having almost certainly produced the largest number of illuminated books and documents and therefore as the site potentially most useful as a source of comparative materials? Or to take as many regional books as possible on grounds that they are more distinctive and therefore more recognizable in making comparisons with other books (or, indeed, more necessary to recognize)? Should borders have been included, then, for their distinctiveness or for their relative lack of distinctiveness? A London/Westminster and a separate regional handbook would have been closer to ideal but was not possible. The resolution to the problem of selection was, first, to try to arrive at a good chronological spread; success in this was less than perfect (see 'Chronological Spread by Decade of Manuscripts Described', p. 126), but was the uppermost criterion if users of this handbook were to have a truly serviceable understanding of English border development and styles in the period. Second, in trying for a mix of London/Westminster and regional books, the selection ended with twelve or thirteen (counting Sheen) metropolitan and twelve regional books, not too unbalanced apart from a preponderance of books from Oxford, not a typical regional site.[21] There were, frankly, a surplus of dated or datable manuscripts with borders from the main production centres of London/Westminster and Oxford, and in order to achieve a full chronological range, manuscripts from these sites were chosen more often than perhaps otherwise justifiable. Ten of the books here have an unknown place of production, which was a lower number than expected. Only two or three manuscripts might have been decorated in a religious house (Pls II, IV, XXXI); several were from a university town, and five (Pls X, XXIX, XXX, XXXIV, XXXVI) might have been products of shops that would take on, if not exclusively, the illumination of royal and other documents, especially in London/Westminster. Since it was the recipients of such documents who apparently paid for the addition of decoration, it has been suggested that they were decorated locally rather than in the place of writing.[22] In my experience, the borders of documents written in the metropolis appear on stylistic grounds to have been illuminated there as well (see e.g. Pls X, XXIX, XXX, XXXIV, XXXVI).

It may have been a problematic decision to include borders that were either reasonably certain to have been made by a non-English craftsman (Pls XXVI, XXXVIIIa) or that may have been made by an English limner closely imitating a foreign style (Pls XVa–b, XXXIX). The decision was, nevertheless, made to include foreign borders (e.g. Pl. XXVI) because of their widespread impact on English limners and because of our need to recognize imitative styles in English books (Pls XVa–b, XXXII, XXXIV). Some foreign artists certainly worked in English shops (Pls xxxviiia–b) and their style, motifs, and border structure must have been observed by English artists.

Plans for this handbook that had to be abandoned were the attempt to trace chronologically the use of a particular border structure or motif in a particular locale, and to trace chronologically general use in England of a particular design such as the trellis border (cf. Pl. ii). Given the inevitable limits of a handbook and the lack of a dated chronological spread of a certain design or motif, this kind of undertaking was not feasible. It was in addition not possible to include a bibliography of reproductions of borders in other dated or datable manuscripts.

My gravest concern for the user of this handbook is, however, that he or she may be tempted to view the selection of borders here as encompassing or definitive. The selection does not reflect the diversity or totality of individual English border artists or even of all styles within the period, and I do not wish the user to feel tacitly encouraged to force a connection between other borders and this selection. This handbook is a guide to styles within a decade or so, with an indication of a few hands within a few regional sites. It contains a fuller demonstration of London/Westminster styles and a reasonably full over-all impression of the chronological development of English designs and motifs between *c.* 1395 and *c.* 1499. It can only as an incidental by-product be used with the forty-three or so border hands reproduced here to identify a particular border hand in another manuscript. The most important outcome would be for the user to develop an eye to the point of being certain that a border made in *c.* 1405 (Pl. v) could not possibly, under any circumstances, have been made *c.* 1435 (Pl. xiv) or *c.* 1455 (Pl. xxv), *c.* 1475 (Pl. xxxi), or, least of all, *c.* 1499 (Pl. xxxix).

Finally, my thanks are due to the many libraries from whose manuscripts the following plates have been drawn. Without such help the production of this handbook would not have been possible.

NOTES

1 I am much indebted to the British Academy for a grant from the Neil Ker Fund, which enabled me to select and describe the dated and datable manuscripts in this handbook.

A number of the terms used in the Introduction are defined in the Glossary, pp. 117–21.

2 I devoted a few pages to the general types of English borders in 'Design, decoration and illustration', in *Book Production and Publishing in Britain 1375–1475*, ed. J. Griffiths and D. Pearsall, Cambridge, 1989, pp. 31–64; and M. Rickert ('Illumination', in *The Text of the Canterbury Tales Studied on the basis of all known manuscripts*, by J. M Manly and E. Rickert, I: Descriptions of the Manuscripts, Chicago, 1940, pp. 561–81) has described, with reproductions,

the borders in Chaucer manuscripts of the *Canterbury Tales*.

3 Because of the possible differences in border style, design, or structure within one manuscript, it was often desirable to reproduce more than one border or a border and spray initial from the same manuscript.

4 There are, however, at least two known sixteenth-century attributions. A note in the Luton Guild Register, f. 121r ('This wrytten & lymmed by John shrppey') apparently refers to the borders for the years 1543–46; and another in the Skinners' Company, London, Book of the Assumption of the Virgin, f. 52r, for work in 1528 (see R. Marks, 'Two Illuminated Guild Registers

from Bedfordshire,' in *Illuminating the Book: Makers and Interpreters; Essays in Honour of Janet Backhouse,* ed. M. P. Brown and S. McKendrick, British Library, London, 1998, pp. 121–41, n. 10). The dated illuminated work in Oxford, St John's College MS 94, Book of Hours, by John Lacy, Newcastle on Tyne, cannot be certainly assigned to one part of the book.

5 As far as documents are concerned, a similar view is expressed by Elizabeth Danbury, who states that all evidence links 'the decoration or illumination on the document very closely to the date given in the dating clause' and that it does 'seem likely. . . that the decoration was added very soon after the document was written in the vast majority of cases'; see Danbury, pp. 163, 162.

6 Flourishwork borders would usefully be the subject of another dated and datable handbook.

7 This kind of border, as in Pl. xxxix, is still planimetric in that all corners are balanced against each other by the same type of acanthus, and each space between is balanced by a flower motif. The illusionistic elements (strewn, naturalistic flowers) have not become part of a 'single perspective view' with the miniature, as discussed by Otto Pächt (*The Master of Mary of Burgundy*, London, 1948, pp. 30–31).

8 In Cambridge, Fitzwilliam Museum MS 2-1954, f. 23v (reproduced in Sandler, *Survey*, II: no. 10, I: ill. 21).

9 See e.g. Sandler, *Survey*, I: ills. 21, 23, 47, 57, 62, 70, 101, 149.

10 See Glossary; or for further discussion and reproductions, see my 'Limning and book-producing terms and signs *in situ* in late-medieval English manuscripts: a first listing', in R. Beadle and A. J. Piper, eds, *New Science out of Old Books: Studies in Manuscripts and Early Printed Books in Honour of A. I. Doyle*, Aldershot and Brookfield, Vermont, 1995), pp. 145–7, 157–8, pls. 22–4, 33–4. Pl. xxx shows a much elongated version of a champ initial, and Pl. xxxia an elongated version of a spray initial. Pl. xxxviiib is a late, squared-off version of a spray initial.

11 It was not possible to discuss all the border types reproduced in the catalogue entries, e.g. Pls. ii, vi.

12 *Ornament*, p. 35.

13 e.g. Sandler, *Survey*, II: no. 101, I: ill. 258.

14 Sandler, *Survey*, II: no. 57, I: ill. 143; II: no. 73, I: ill. 185.

15 Scott, *Survey*, II: no. 9, I: ills. 48, 50, 51, 56; Janet Backhouse, *The Sherborne Missal*, The British Library, London 1999, especially pls. 6, 21, 38, 42, 53, and endpiece, p. 64.

16 Scott, *Survey*, II: no. 48, I: ill. 199.

17 Scott, *Survey*, II: no. 79, I: ill. 305, and ff. 12v, 15v, 19v, 95v, etc.; see also BL Harley MS 2278, f. 6 (Scott, *Survey*, II: no. 78, I: ill. 311).

18 This Master however decorated a document and two manuscripts in England dated, respectively, 1447, 1448, and 1450; see Scott, *Survey*, II: no. 100, I: ills. 378–80, 411.

19 New York, Public Library, MS Spencer 3, Pt. II, *c.* 1450 – before 1467 (Scott, *Survey*, II: no. 106, I: ill. 398); BL Harley MS 2887, before 1467 (Scott, *Survey*, II: no. 109, I: ill. 402); New York, Public Library, MS Glazier 9, *c.* 1450–60 (Scott, *Survey*, II: no. 108, ff. 14v, 41, 45v, 50, etc.); Oxford, Bodl. MS Digby 227, dated 1461 (Scott, *Survey*, II: no. 101a, ills. 382–3).

20 The angels and birds in Cambridge, Fitzwilliam Museum 3-1979, are an exception (Scott, *Survey*, II: no. 80, I: ills 316-7).

21 A number of other dated Oxford borders are described and reproduced in my 'Two Sequences of Dated Illuminated Manuscripts made in Oxford 1450–64', in J. P. Carley and C. G. C. Tite, eds, *Books and Collectors 1200–1700; Essays presented to Andrew Watson*, The British Library, London, 1997, pp. 43–69.

22 E. Danbury states that the illumination of documents in this period was mainly paid for by the beneficiaries (p. 160) and that in consequence the illumination was of high quality (p. 178). She also feels that the illumination was probably done 'in many cases locally' (p. 168), that is, in the region of the beneficiary/ies. Such a situation would account for a diversity of style but not necessarily a high quality of workmanship.

Plate Ia Roger Dymok, *Liber contra duodecim errores*
    & hereses Lollardorum, 1395–99

Plate XVIII *Nova statuta Angliae, c.* 1445/6

Plate XXXII Luton Guild Register, 1475

19

Plate XXXIX William Parron, *De astrorum vi fatali*, 1499–1500

DATED & DATABLE
ENGLISH MANUSCRIPT BORDERS

ABBREVIATIONS

Bk.	Book	MS	Manuscript
BL	British Library, London	M.E.	Middle English
Bodl.	Bodleian Library, Oxford	*n.b.*	*nota bene*
Bp	Bishop	N.T.	New Testament
cm.	centimetre(s)	O.T.	Old Testament
c.	*circa*	p./pp.	page/pages
cf.	compare	Pl./Pls	Plate/Plates
col./cols	column/columns	prob.	probably
Com.	Company	PRO	Public Record Office
CUL	Cambridge University Library	r	recto
		R.	right
EWV	Early Wycliffite Version	ref./refs	reference/references
Ed.	Edward	Rich.	Richard
Eng.	English	St	Saint
ERO	Essex Record Office	*S.C.*	*Summary Catalogue* of the Bodleian Library
f./ff.	folio/folios		
Fr.	French	UL	University Library
Hen.	Henry	v	verso
incl.	including	V & A Lib.	Victoria & Albert Museum, National Art Library
LWV	Later Wycliffite Version		
L.	left	wr.	written at/by
Lat.	Latin	?	a probable limning site
membr.	membrane		

Although measurements are often given to the nearest millimetre, they must be taken as only approximate, given the irregularity of the vellum concerned.

Cambridge, Trinity Hall, MS 17. Roger Dymok, *Liber contra duodecim errores & hereses Lollardorum* (Lat. and Eng.). Dedicated to Rich. II, with portrait, arms and badges.

Datable: early 1395 (text wr.)–Sept 1399 (Rich. II in captivity)

Description: parchment; ii + 160 + i; ff. 26.5 × 18.8 cm. Ruling in rose ink. Red and blue paraphs. In red: text, running titles, and titles; capitals tinted yellow. Some ascenders with profile heads. 4-line blue letters with red infilling with a 1-sided flourishwork border in red and blue, usually with a leaf, animal mask, or profile head in a roundel; 3-sided border with coloured letter on gold ground infilled with vines and leaves, f. 81r. Three full borders, three historiated initials, ff. 1r (Rich. II enthroned), 5r (John the Baptist), 14r (emperor and saint).

Borders: f. 5r. [see opposite and the colour plate, page 17] This full border is typical of a four-sided border of this period, if less grand than the first in the manuscript. The text is framed by a double bar composed of a vine coloured in alternating sections of rose and blue beside a continuous gold stippled bar. The right corners are expanded to contain interlaces, above, in a circular shape with loops around a center circle (see Cover), and, below, a diagonal with small ending loops on an engrailed and gold base. The left corners are enlarged by coloured leaves and gold spike motifs.

The L. bar-frame is elaborated with pairs of leaves, an interwoven vine and pointed gold filler-motifs, a design typical of the late 14th century. The design at the R. mid-point is that of two vine roundels enclosing a single leaf, from which develop vines and sprays with coloured holly and trefoil leaves and gold balls. This vine- and spray-work-design was used, with only slight modification, throughout the following century. Here the vines disappear illusionistically under a gold base and continue to the end of the spray (see Cover), unlike later sprays of penwork (Pls XIV, XX). The only penwork on this border are squiggles on gold balls and short lines between coloured motifs. The pigments are rose, blue, and dull orange, and all the gold surfaces are stippled with rows of dots. The motifs here, as generally in the next century, are outlined in black ink.

The historiation shows a possibly unique iconography of John the Baptist preaching to six listeners (see Cover). The curve of the letter is notable for its monochrome twist or cable pattern, and the stem for a simple wavy line and a row of dots and circles.

Plate Ia Roger Dymok, *Liber contra duodecim errores & hereses Lollardorum*, full bar-frame border with mid-column bar

f. 81r. This page has two borders, one in pigments and gold and the other in red and blue flourishwork (R. col.). The motifs are again typical of the period, e.g. the undifferentiated single leaf in the upper spray, the triangular leaf at its end, the pair of holly leaves beside the initial I, and the rounded trefoil leaf at the end of the lower spray. Of these only the holly and curled leaves continue to be used in the 15th century (cf. Pl. VIII near initial). The curled leaf motif in the lower spray may be an innovation in this book. The fine I – of an orange interlace on a gold ground, creating a trellis effect – is rarely seen after *c.* 1400–1405.

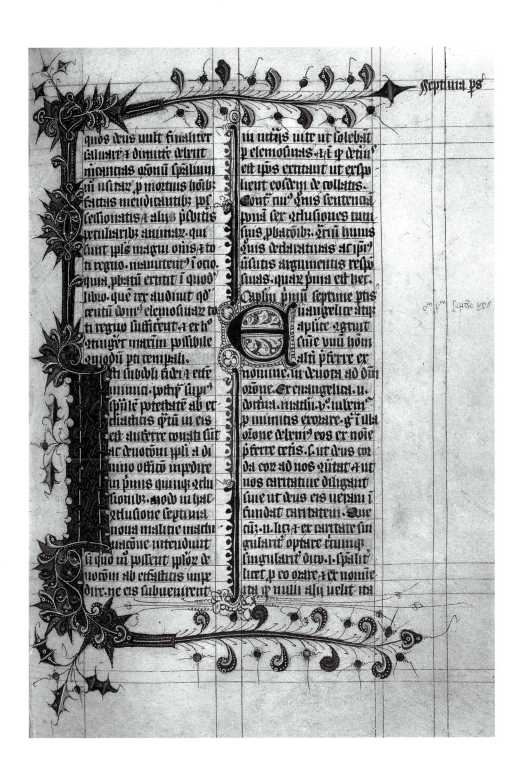

Plate Ib Roger Dymok, *Liber contra duodecim errores & hereses* 25
    Lollardorum, (L.) bar-and-spray border and (R.) flourishwork border

Oxford, Bodleian Library, MS Bodley 316 (*S.C.* 2752). Ff. 2r–150r, Ranulf Higden, *Polychronicon*; ff. 152r–75r, Thomas Walsingham, Chronicle of England, 1328–1388 (Lat.); etc.

Datable: after *c.* 1394 (ref. to contemporary event)–1397 (donated before death of Thomas of Woodstock), ?Norwich (?Benedictine house)

Description: parchment; 183 ff.; 35.8 × 25.7 cm. Red underlining. Red and blue paraphs. 3-line blue letters with red flourishing; 6-line red and blue parted letters with leaves in reservework and red and purple flourishing. One border (with coat of arms and angel supporters), one border figure (kneeling religious in lavender habit), and one historiated initial, f. 8r (Crucifix-Trinity).

Border: f. 8r. The border that introduces this copy of the *Polychronicon* is typical not only of its period but probably also of a production site that may be Benedictine and possibly Norwich (Scott, *Survey*) and that produced more than one copy of the same text. The border is four-sided with a central bar between the text columns, wrapped with leaves. The basic frame, at top, of a single bar of rose and blue on a stippled gold ground (possibly a design that preceeded the later, standard coloured bar with a gold bar beside it) is elaborated at L. by a band of alternating panels of rose and blue with white filigreework, and at bottom and R. by a broader band of two vines on a gold base separated and infilled with various coloured motifs. This last design is called a trellis border.

At the upper right corner a winged dragon functions as cornerpiece. Below the dragon and on which it apparently rests is a caryatid-like leaf or flower motif with a face superimposed. Between it and the lower corner two vines act as a support for large acanthus leaves whose lobes seem to clutch around the vines. At the R. mid-point and lower corner are interlaces, a very common design for a cornerpiece; the lower design incorporates a lion mask. The lower band border is more obviously trelliswork in that vines loop in circles back and forth between the bars, enclosing large maple-like leaves. Four columbines of dark lavender hang from the outside of the gold band, possibly a badge or indication of the house or order (?Benedictine) where the book was produced. The colours used in the border are deep rose, blue, and orange.

Other characteristics typical of this kind of attractive late 14th-century border are pairs of daisy buds and pairs of kite or other leaves at L. and top; rounded three-lobed leaves (of two kinds) at R.; and the non-modelled manner of shading by straight lines, round white areas, and rows of dots. Elaboration at two corners of the initial by roundels of vines enclosing leaves is customary, as is the rounded shaded work in white on the letter.

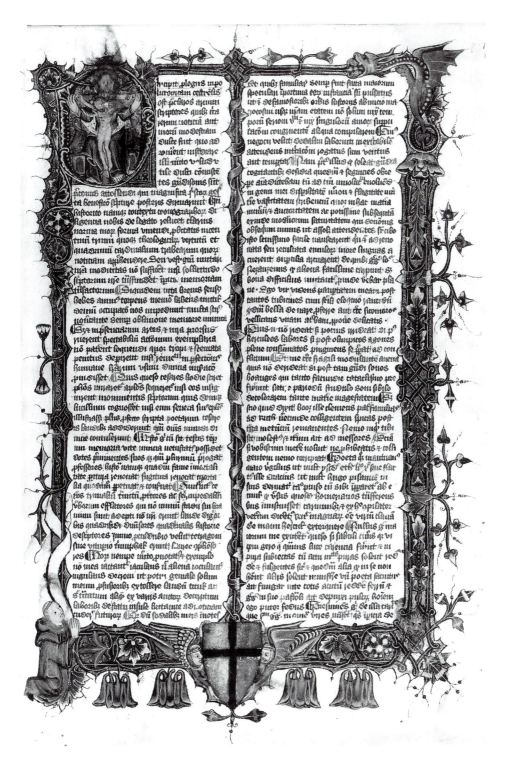

Plate II Ranulf Higden, *Polychronicon*,
mixed bar and trellis border with mid-column bar

London, British Library, Harley MS 401. *Floretum evangelicum.*

Dated: 1396: f. 334r: 'Explicit floret<u>um</u> anno doⁱ. 1396'.

Description: parchment; 334 ff.; 20.8 × 14.5 cm. In red: underlining; stroked capitals; *nota bene* hands; blue or red and blue paraffs. 2-line blue letters with red flourishing; alternating in the Table of Contents with gold letters with red flourishing; 2-, 3-, or 4-line gold letters on rose/blue ground with sprays. Two borders, ff. 1r, 75r; one marginal miniature, f. 334v (two hands in nebuly).

Borders: f. 1r. The illuminated decoration in this manuscript is conventional in having only two borders and in their positions, at the Table of Contents and at the first text page. A design in which both borders are three-sided is less typical: it is more common to find one full and one partial border (Pls XXXIa, b). The L. frame is made up one bar of gold decorated with a row of stippled dots and one bar of alternating panels in rose and blue with a rope-twist design in white. From the bar and from engrailed points on the initial ground emerge sprigs of two or three daisy buds on black pen lines; and red and blue balls with pen squiggles are laid against the bar. The sprays are composed of black pen lines that support pairs of daisy buds and end in a single bud. The sprays do not reach across to the end of the text space, unlike usual practice in the 15th century (Pls XIV, XXIb, etc.)

The daisy bud motif is typical of later 14th-century borders, if more usually as pairs on a sprig rather than on a spray. The calyx of the buds is of a wash green, with rose used at the tips of the un-opened petals.

Plate IIIa *Floretum evangelicum*, Table of Contents page, partial border

F. 7r. This more elaborate border connects to a partial figure letter made from the hindquarters, leg, and wing of a grotesque (see Detail) and from a letter stem which is blue, shaded and hatched in white with white circles along the inner side of the stem. Above the initial, a curled leaf leads to a blue vine that supports pairs of rose and blue trefoils and gold balls. Below, the initial leads to a bar frame that ends at bottom in a curled leaf. The leaf initiates another vine (in rose) that lies on a triangular panel of blue framed in gold; the vine again supports pairs of trefoils and balls.

Characteristic traits of these two late 14th-century borders are: colouring limited to dark rose and bright blue; vines on a panel; trefoils with two rounded lobes and with the third elongated and pointed; a panel at R. beside the initial; a grotesque; coloured balls laid against a gold base; a circle of white on leaves (here in the initial); and the initial I (f. 1r) not ruled into the text space (Pl. IIIa).

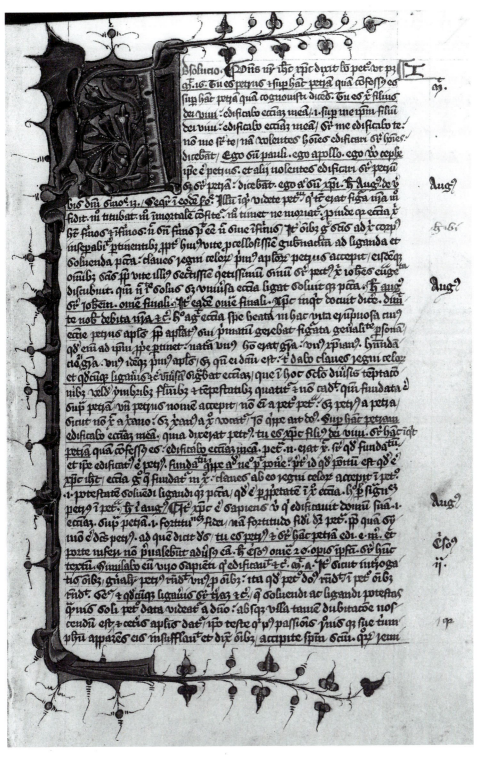

Plate IIIb *Floretum evangelicum*, first text page, three-sided border 31

Eton, College Library MS. 108. [2 MSS] Ff. 1r–110v, St Augustine, *De Trinitate*; ff. 112r–185v, William Norton, *Tabula super doctorem de lyra*; etc.

Date: [ff. 112r–185v] 1403: f. 185v, 'Explicit tabula. . . compilata et scripta per Fratrem Willelmum Morton de sacro ordine Fratrum minorum in conuentu Couentrey. Anno domini Mᵒ CCCCᵐᵒ tercio etc.'

Description: parchment; 190 ff.; 30.3 × 22 cm. In red: signatures, running titles. Red and blue paraphs. Decorated ascenders and descenders. 2-, 3-, 4-, and 5-line blue letters flourished in red. One border; one historiated initial, f. 112r (lion mask with leaves).

Border: f. 112r. This border is instructive as an example of a common border design in the earliest period of the 15th century. It contains motifs also used in the late 14th century but lacks any of the new elements of borders made as soon as two years later (Pl. V). Designs retained from the previous century are: (i) short vines that commence inside the bar-frame and end outside in a pair of leaves separated by a gold ball with squiggles (Pl. Ia, upper border); (ii) a rectangular base from which the vine and leaf sprig begins; (iii) interlaces at mid-points (Pl. II); and (iv) strong white bands of shading on leaf motifs (Pls Ia, II). The infilling of the initial with a lion mask and the stippled areas of gold are typical of both the late 14th and early 15th centuries.

The colour range is still kept to rose and blue, with only the lion's head and one pair of leaves in orange. It is early in the century and not surprising to find quite small roundels (of only four or five leaves) as the cornerpieces and only a few single leaves just outside the initial ground. There is no feathering or true spraywork on the bar-frame as a mere two years later in the borders of Harley 2946 (Pl. V); two short sprays of coloured leaves and gold balls however project into the space between the two columns, with leaves still in the style and rendering of those in Pl. I. This is a competent but essentially utilitarian border design that may have been used as minimal decoration in books that were to have only one or two borders.

Although stated by one of the scribes as written in a Coventry house, the border style gives no particular clue to the origin of the artist's hand. The slightly retrograde motifs and lack of new ones may only indicate an earlier date of training. There is some doubt about the date of the border in that a similar inscription occurs in Bodl. MS Laud Misc. 156 and other manuscripts as by 'Norton' (which may be the more accurate version of the compiler's name), and Eton 108 may be a copy of another manuscript. If this is the date of the compilation and not that of the Eton manuscript, the style of the Eton border nevertheless agrees with the date of *c.* 1403.

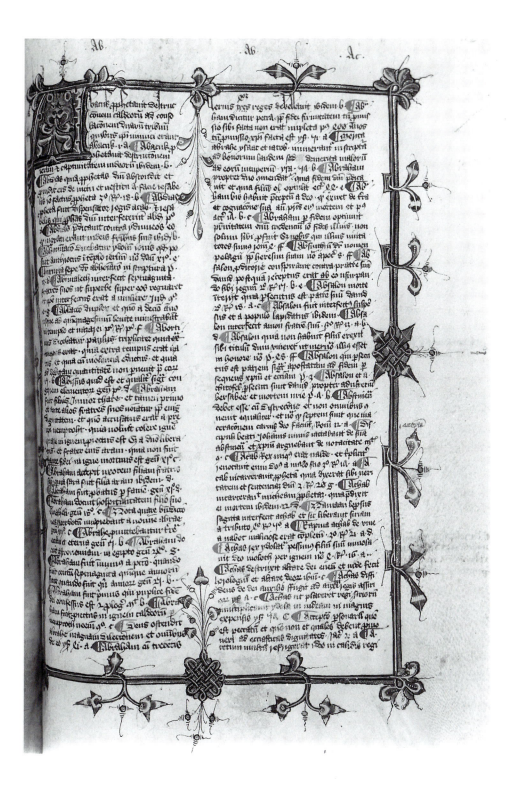

Plate IV William Norton, *Tabula super doctorem de lyra*,
full bar-frame border

33

London, British Library, Harley MS 2946. Breviary (Lat. & Eng.).

Date: 1405, wr. by T. F: f. 420v, 'Iste liber scriptus fuit per/T.ff. Anno domini Millo C°C°C°C° quinto'.

Description: parchment; 429 ff.; 18.8 × 12.9 cm. In red: text; line endings. 1-line red and blue capitals; 2-line blue letters with red flourishing; 4- and 5-line gold letters on a muted rose and blue quartered ground with white designs. One 2-sided bar border with sprays in two margins, f. 244r; two full bar borders, ff. 1r, 181r; one miniature, f. 181r (David with harp).

Border: f. 181r. This full border is first recognizable as of its period through its overall sparseness of motif by contrast with the more extensive spraywork and use of motifs of later decades. There are at the same time important changes in this border by comparison with the previous full bar border (Pl. IV). The cornerpieces are more prominent, the row of leaves above the initial is more extensive, and sinuous sprays range outside the R. and lower frames. These are designs that will be developed throughout the century, whereas the interlace and short sprays of the previous border are largely dropped from the limning stock of motifs. The roundels at three corners here are formed by coloured leaves alternating with pointed gold designs (an older feature) and are infilled by three leaves of the same nondescript type. Single leaves seem to sprout from the vine of the bar frame; and gold balls with pen squiggles float unattached to the frame (at top), a motif that persists until *c.* 1420 (Pl. VIII). The colour range is, like the previous border, limited to (muted) rose and blue. The penwork in the sprays and on the gold balls is black, and no lobes are drawn on the feathering nor green tint used, as in later manuscripts.

The letter of the historiated initial is halved horizontally between a bright blue and orange with designs in white and a wavy line at the outer edge; it is marked with short strokes in white rather than shaded and at the inner sides with rows of dots and circles. A circle of rose marked with a white cross is set into the gold base of the initial ground.

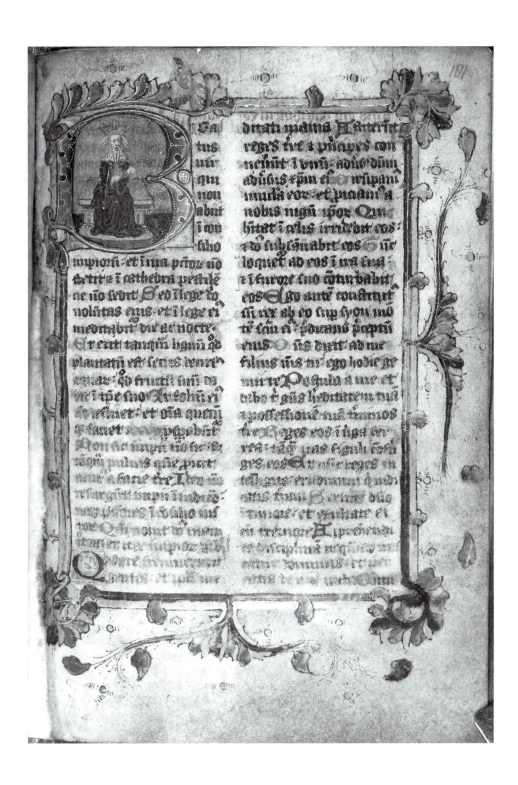

Plate Va Breviary, full bar-frame border

F. 244r. This secondary border is an example of a design used in the 14th and early 15th centuries more frequently than in the rest of the 15th: its chief characteristic is a bar frame on two sides ending in a coloured vine and spray-work that almost meets to form a full border. While the frame, leaf roundels, and uncoloured feathering are like the previous border, this border has a further element: a pair of tightly curled leaves (on the L. bar) of a type possibly introduced in Trinity Hall 17 (Pl. I). The pointed vines leading to the spraywork and the gold engrailed base will soon be replaced by a spray of penwork feathering.

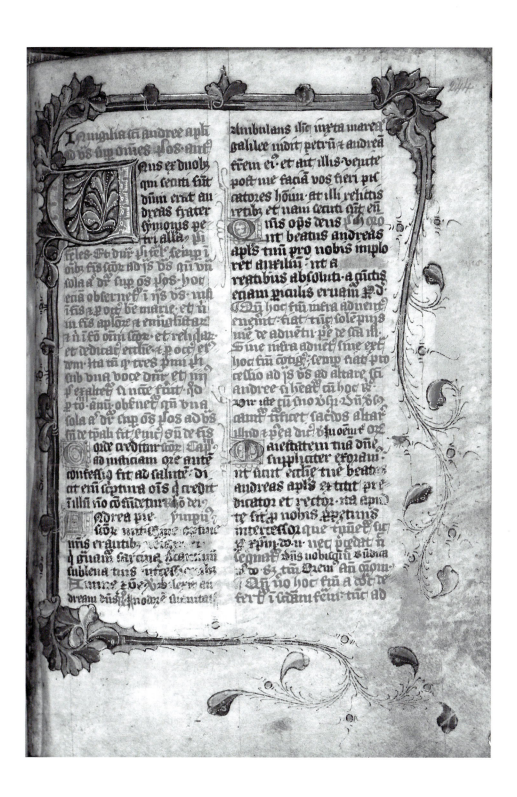

Plate Vb Breviary, partial bar frame and spray border

Oxford, Bodleian Library, MS Laud Lat. 4. Ff. 1r–147r, John of Salisbury, *Polycraticus*; ff. 148–182v, C. Julius Solinus, *De mirabilibus mundi*; ff. 183–199v, Eutropius, *Brevarium historiae Romanorum*; ff. 200r–271v, Orosius, *De ormesta seu miseria mundi*.

Dated: 1406 (f. v^v), wr. by John Merylynch [or Moorlinch], monk of the Benedictine abbey, Glastonbury: ff. 147r, 182v, 199v, 271v, '. . .perquisitus et scriptus per fratrem Johannem merylynche monachum Glastonie'.

Description: parchment; i + 273 (f. 49 twice) ff.; 37.5 × 24.5 cm. In red: marginal names. 1-line blue capitals with red flourishing; 2- or 3- line blue letters with red flourishing; 5-line parted red and blue letters with red flourishing with 3-sided flourishwork border. Six borders (some cut).

Border: f. 66v. This full border has three sides of a bar frame border (top, L., and mid-col.) and two of a band border (c. 7mm wide) with panels of alternating rose and blue. The panels are decorated with various white designs (rows of circles, shell patterns, and curving acanthus leaves), which are interrupted by smaller sections of gold with interlaces, a group of three leaves, a sprig of two or three leaves, or a single trefoil leaf; from the gold panels extend a sprig of two or three leaves, sometimes with a gold ball with curved finishing lines. The interlaces, although relatively simple, are of three different designs. The cornerpieces are, apart from the upper L. site, a vine roundel with simple leaves around the outside and one or more leaves on the inside on a gold background, a design in use until at least 1430 (cf. Pl. XIII) and occasionally later. The mid-column bar shows pairs of simple or curled leaves, with two more elaborate breaks in the bar by half-roundels of leaves at the mid-points between the initial and the upper and lower frames. The four-line initial also has two small roundels of leaves at two corners, with four leaves curling in a vine inside the letter E.

The design of a band, used as part or all of a border, is typical of the later 14th and early 15th centuries, as is the range of colour limited to rose, blue, and gold. The white shadings in bands and a relatively large circle on leaves are also indicative of this early period. The motifs and the frame are outlined by a firm black line, which is also used for the pen lines. There is no spraywork and only a few curving lines on this border: it is stiff, with even the external sprigs in a rigid formation in contrast to the border of the previous year. Like the border shown on Pl. IV, this border has none of the 'modern' elements of the border on Pl. V; but such differences in design coexisted because of different periods of training of artists and their accessibility to changes in fashion.

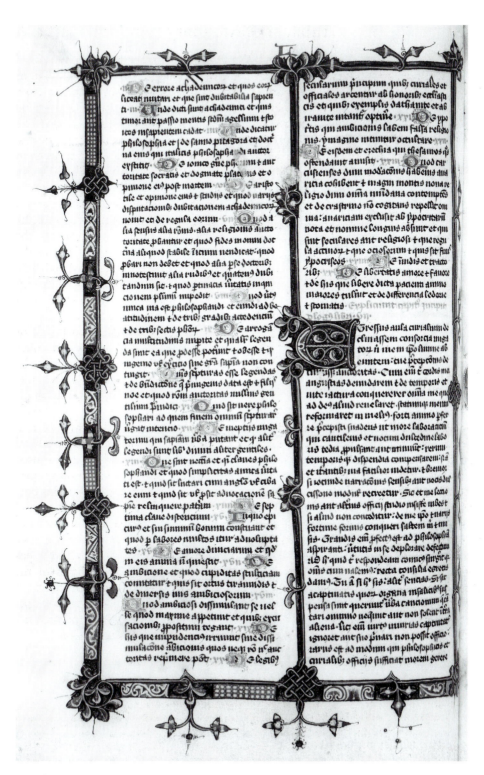

Plate VI John of Salisbury, *Polycraticus*,
mixed band and bar border, with mid-column bar

Oxford, Bodleian Library, MS Fairfax 2 (*S.C.* 3882). Wycliffite Bible (N. T., LWV; O.T., EWV).

Date: 1408: f. 385r: 'Here ende# #e apocalips/#e eer[sic] of #e lord M. CCC[C] & viij #is book was endid'.

Description: parchment; 390 ff.; 42.8 × 28 cm. In red: underlining, paraffs, running titles. 2- and 5-line blue letters with red flourishing. Two borders, ff. 1r, 3r.

Border: f. 1r. The introductory border in this manuscript is three-sided, with a bar-frame at L. that develops at top and bottom into a row of aligned leaves as cornerpieces. The vine and row of leaves at top and bottom curve outward before developing into a straight vine that ends in spraywork. This standard design is shown here in two stages: the upper vine extends out past the gold base before becoming penwork, whereas the lower vine ends at the end of the gold base and immediately turns into pen spraywork. The latter design prevails during the rest of the century, and the upper design is indicative of an earlier fashion. The penwork or feathering supports matched pairs of leaves and gold balls.

At about the mid-point of the text space, the L. vertical frame makes a sudden convex curve, a standard element of bar design in the early part of this period. Also typical, the bar has either a single leaf or a cluster of three leaves sprouting from it; interspersed between them on the bar are gold balls with pen squiggles. The single leaf is used into the 1450s as the point of departure for sprays (cf. Pl. XX). With this border the earlier stiffness is relieved by the curl at the end of the lower spray and by the curvilinear shape of the corners, but the upper spray does not have the fluidity even of the sprays of about three years earlier in Pl. V, suggesting an artist in transition between styles.

The six-line initial is of gold on a quartered rose/blue ground, with white filigreework outside the letter and a white reservework design of vines and leaves created inside by hatching. The red flourishing visible beneath and below the initial suggests either that the flourisher mistakenly entered an initial where an illuminated letter was intended or that there was a contemporary change of plan concerning the first page.

Characteristic of the period before and around (but not long after) 1408 are: a curved row of leaves on a gold ground at corners; straight sprays with pairs of leaves; sprigs of paired leaves on the lower edge of the lower gold base; leaves with round white circles as shading; a curve at the mid-point on a bar, especially in larger manuscripts; feathering without green colouring; and rather crude trefoil leaves with striations and a circle.

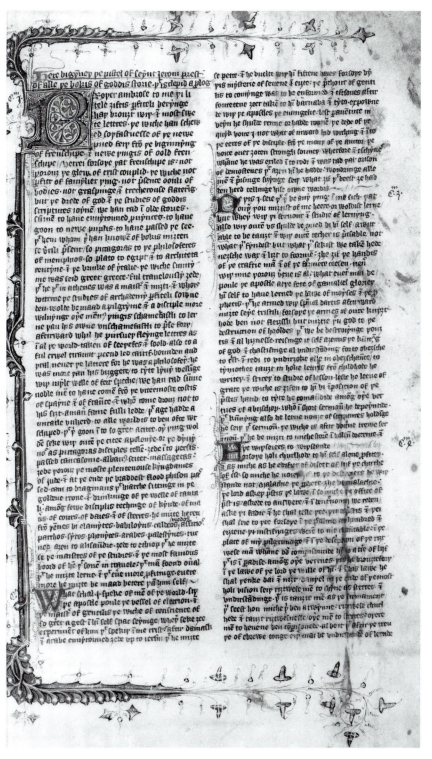

Plate VII Wycliffite Bible, three-sided border

London, British Library, Arundel MS 38. Thomas Hoccleve, *Regiment of Princes* (Eng. and Lat.).

Datable: not before 1410 (on internal refs to execution of a Lollard) – not after 1413 (ref. to Hen. V as Prince of Wales), prob. London or Westminster.

Description: parchment; 99 ff.; 29.2 × 18.5 cm. 1-line blue and gold paraffs with red and lavender flourishing. One 2-line gold letter on a rose/blue ground with sprigs; one 3- to 4-line blue letter on a gold ground with sprays. Thirteen 3-sided borders; one pictorial text insertion, f. 65r (man pulling stanza into place by rope); one miniature, f. 37r (young man presenting book to prince).

Border: f. 86v. This three-sided border with a bar frame at L. and sprays in the upper and lower margins combines both older and newer elements of decoration. Particularly anachronistic is the row of coloured leaves that begins inside the bar-frame and curves over the top of it to finish in a near circle in the margin. Other older features are the sprigs (at corners and mid-points), each composed of two gold balls, a gold trefoil, and tinted pen squiggles; and the short rows of deeply curled, single leaves (cf. Pl. Ib) that develop from two initial corners. The range of colour is limited to rose and blue, with occasional dabs of orange for a leaf.

A newer element here is the trumpet motif that rationalizes the point of development of the vine from the initial corners and that appears in two sprays. But, most important, are the large acanthus leaves with spiky lobes outlined in black at the upper and lower ends of the bar. Although the tip of these acanthus leaves is used here to act as the origin of the spraywork, this type of leaf soon became an end in itself and a favourite theme in at least one London shop of *c.* 1410–1425. Also new is the green tint on pen squiggles. The final element that shows this border to be current and probably from a London/Westminster shop is the finely rendered, monochrome leaf within the initial. The book is assigned to the metropolis, then, on stylistic grounds.

Like many other 15th-century borders, full and partial, this border presents different motifs on different sprays, here (above) holly leaves and (below) simple leaves without lobes and one trumpet. The other borders in this book offer further examples of the range of coloured (kites, kidneys) and monochrome (e.g. ff. 39v, 66, 73) motifs and of the spiky (ff. 39v, 60v, 63) acanthus used at this period.

This border design was employed in other Hoccleve manuscripts and was apparently found more appropriate to verse stanzas than a full four-sided border. In this manuscript not even the first border is four-sided, though its sprays contain considerably more coloured motifs (at top, nine; at bottom, eleven) than this border, and its bars are wrapped with illusionistic scrollwork.

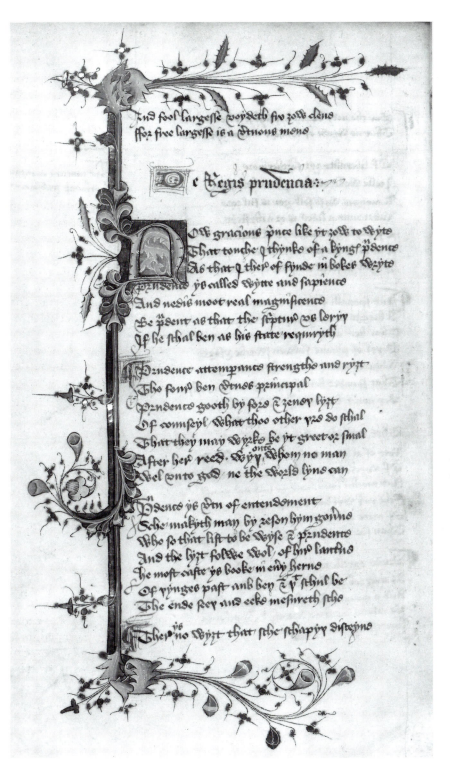

Plate VIII Thomas Hoccleve, *Regiment of Princes*, three-sided border

43

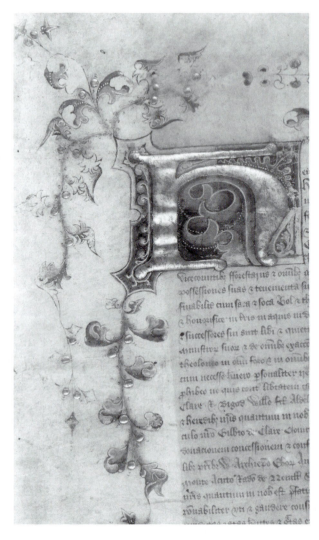

1416, Westminster

Plate IX

Chelmsford, Essex Record Office, Maldon Borough Records, D/B 3/13/7. Inspeximus and confirmation of a charter of 31 Edward III.

Date: 5 November 4 Hen. V [=1416], wr. Westminster, by Kays.

Description: parchment; 1 membr.; 55.6 × 34.3 cm. 1-line gold letters; one large initial. One border.

Border: top & L. of document. [The document could be examined only under a heavy plastic covering.] This expert spray border begins directly from the engrailed corners of an impressive introductory initial. The letter **h** ['henricus'], of gold without pricking, lies on a quartered deep rose (maroon) and blue ground, infilled with a deeply folded and modelled acanthus leaf with a spine

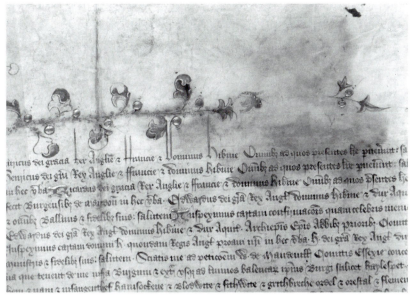

of white dots. The leaf, like the background, is quartered between the two colours. On the R. exterior ground of the letter the design consists of stylized two-dimensional acanthus leaves: (above) a frontal leaf that extends along the curve of the letter and (below) a profile leaf with smaller lobes, both shaded and outlined in white. On the L. ground the single leaves curled into a ball form are given three-dimensional shading.

The spraywork borders that extend along each side of the text are lively, almost 'pretty' in their drawing and execution. The main vines are still straight compared with some earlier spraywork (Pls V, VIII), but the colouring is a bright green and the leaf motifs seem to be full of energy: they arch backwards and the upper lobe then curls forward over the front of the leaf; and they are staggered on the vine, creating a less stiff effect. All three sprays end in a sprig of three smaller leaves of an older style (some are rubbed). The leaf colouring is of a bright blue similar to that of the initial and of a rose lighter than the initial.

Gold balls are placed close to the main vine and have only one squiggle in a pale brown ink. The feathering is composed of tiny lobes and drawn in pale brown ink also close to the main vine, which is coloured with one long stroke of green. The diagonal spray from the upper L. corner of the initial has leaves that are more pointed and more angular in their reversal on themselves; this spray also has (upper R.) a sprig of kidney leaves, only beginning to be used in the first decade of this century and perhaps derived from a rounder leaf of the previous century.

Although both artists used the deeply folded acanthus as infilling for an initial, the graceful style of the border here is somewhat ahead of the sprays in Arundel 38. The three-lobed leaf folded back on itself and the large gold balls were used in Cambridge, Corpus Christi College, MS 61 and in books made for John Whetehamstede (Scott, *Survey*); and the occurrence of these motifs here seems to be an early instance of the style in a (presumably) London/Westminster shop.

Plate IX Inspeximus and confirmation of a charter of 31 Edward III

London, British Library, Harley Charters 51.H.6. Inspeximus concerning Tateshale and Seremby Hall, Kirkeby, Lincs. [damaged]

Date: 20 March 9 Hen. V [=1421/2], wr. Westminster, by Nicholas Wymbyssh, clerk: end of text '. . .apud Westmonasterium vicesimo die marcij Anno regni nostri nono' [Humfrey, duke of Gloucester noted as 'custode Anglie'].

Description: parchment; 1 membr.; 59.8 × 88.5 cm. Flourished ascenders. One border, one historiated initial (seated king, Henry VI, with sceptre).

Border: top and L. of document. This spraywork border, made of the same type of spraywork that is a constituent of a bar border, originates directly from the large introductory initial. This design seems to have been preferred for documents (cf. Pls IX, XXIX, XXXIV), even if they may also appear with other kinds of texts (Pls XXVI, XXXIa). The upper spray contains only three-lobed leaves as coloured motifs, and the side spray L. (at top) contains three aroid flowers whose leaves and centre are quite flattened. The lowest three flowers have a three-pointed calyx, are more graceful, and show a larger, more rounded aroid center. The four remaining aroid motifs are unusual in having a worm- or carrot-like center, two of green and one of orange, with the supporting leaves flattened at right angles to the centre. The various gold motifs comprise a spiky trefoil, a rounded trefoil, and the usual gold balls with pen squiggles. The black feathering is curling in design. Like the tones of the initial letter, the colours of rose, blue and green used in the spraywork are abnormally darkened. The twisted illusionistic acanthus in the letter stems is notable, especially in contrast to earlier letter-stem decoration (Pls V, VIII).

This border is important for three of the coloured motifs, each of them aroids. The flower nearest in design to the flattened aroid is a frontal view of an aroid in Lambeth Palace MS 474, f. 72r, of c. 1415, which would appear flattened if rendered from the side. The period of introduction of the flattened aroid is therefore likely to be between c. 1415 and c. 1420. The worm-like aroid is not known until the present document and may well be an import from a French shop such as that of the Boucicaut Master, c. 1410 (cf. Paris, Musée Jacquemart-André MS 2), but whether an import or invention of this artist, c. 1420 is probably its date of entry into the English repertoire of aroid motifs. This is also the first dated instance of the trumpet-shaped aroid (upper L. roundel of initial). The aroid motif was apparently much admired, for it is found in extensive use through the next three to four decades in England.

Plate X Inspeximus concerning Tateshale and Seremby Hall, Lincs.

47

Dominica tertius diñ euãgð rxbuj

Aria magdalena t maria
iacobi t salome emerunt
aromata vt venientes vn
gent ihm t c. ayt 16. Nos
andem p experiencia qð qui
quilibz delectat in psencia
illius quem diligit. t si p ait absens si
assit possibilitas ipm diligere inquirit
inquirens aut diligere id cum affect t de
sidio magno si plus invenit qn spabat
tur in ipso augmentat gaudiu qm in illo
invento amplius sepit. Exempli gracia
si quis queret centu libras cum mag
no desidio. t nusso sepiret tantu augue
tat in ipso gaudiu qm a3. centu excedero
cmosaret. Qua igit isto sco mulieres
deuotissime qui xpm hebant psentem
quia ipm diligebant delectabant in eius
psencia qn fuerit eis absens ipm qsieit
cum magno desidio t affect. Qua q ipm
querebant in monumento iacente t mor
tuu. t ipm invenirut iam resuscitatid t
vivum. tantu potuit cumulari in eis gau
diu qm vivus excessit mortuu. t qm sco
su excessit passibile. t mortale. t hoc
est quod nobis testat histo euãgelij ho
diern in quo luculente dicit cuiigeta q
vndit. auiditate inquisicois amoroso. no
uitaten apicois gisoz. sublimitatem
condicois giioso. celsitudinen legacois
gaudioz. Primu pbat obsequij sedu
litas. 2m angeli claritas. 3m loci vacuitas.
t festi celebritas. P in pna. 2m ibi Et
introeuntes in monumictu. t 3m ibi Qui
dixit illis. nolite expauesce t c. qm ibi S

1425, ?Lincoln

Plate XI

Cambridge, University Library, MS. Gg.4.19. Philip de Monte Calerio, *Postilla super evangelia dominicalia*, Pt. II (Lat.).

Date: finished 10 May 1425, wr. by John Weston, Lincoln: f. 291r, 'Hic liber quo ad scripturam finitus est per gratiam patris & filii & spiritus sancti per Joh. Weston de linc' scriptorem X° die maij Anno dni millo CCCC^{mo} XXV° & A° h. Reg' vj tercio'.

Description: parchment; 291 ff.; 35.5 × 25.6 cm. Running titles; capitals with yellow tint. 2- and 4-line blue letters with red flourishing. One border, f. 2r.

Border: f. 2r. The text begins with a six-line letter (**M**) coloured in blue with white shading along the outside of the letter and with a row of white dots and a circle on the inside of the stems. The letter is infilled in each section with an elongated acanthus leaf in blue with several lobes in another colour. Both leaves develop from the lower part of the letter, and the letter also starts vines that lead into the marginal decoration. These two aspects of the initial and vine design are known from at least the late 14th century, and these organic connections between initial infilling and/or bar-frame continue to be drawn until later in the 15th century (cf. Pl. XXXII).

Sprays are in the upper and L. margins only and take their beginning from the same vine that began in the initial; here it passes with rows of leaves over a gold base, and ends in a point. At top, the vine disappears illusionistically beneath its gold base to reappear as the support for feathering work. The motifs in the upper spray are paired gold balls, here together with paired leaves coloured in pink, blue, green, and a murky orange and deeply curled to form a circular shape. The upper spray ends with a simple leaf turned back on itself, in a form reminiscent of much earlier borders.

The L. spray begins from two rows of leaves with curled tips and a murky orange vine. The motifs in the feathering are small rounded green lobes, gold balls, and unusual coloured motifs composed of four overlapping ?petals without an aroid center.

The rendering and presence of the rows of leaves, the deeply curled leaves, the folded-over ending leaf (see above), the green vine of the sprays (rather than penwork feathering; cf. Pl. X), and the straightness of the vine and spray are indicative of a border designed in the previous decade – but here more likely of a limner trained at that time. It may also indicate a provincial (?Lincoln) but still professional site of limning.

Glasgow, University Library, MS Hunter 215 (U.2.6). *Cartularium Prioratus Sanctae Trinitatis infra Aldgate* ('Aldgate Cartulary'), London.

Datable: 1425–27, prob. London (on grounds of destination); f. 8r, wr. by canon Thomas de Axbridge.

Description: parchment; 208 ff.; 33.1 × 23.5 cm. Decorated ascenders. Red and blue paraphs. 1-line red and blue capitals; 2- or 3-line blue letters with red flourishing, some with heads; 4-, 5-, 6-, and 7-line letters on a gold ground, infilled with (i) vines and leaves or (ii) monochrome scrolled acanthus, with spraywork. One partial border, f. 149r; one full border and historiated initial (coat of arms), f. 1r; one marginal tinted drawing, f. 150r (bust of a bishop).

Border: f. 1r. The decoration of this border is scanty for work at this period: motifs are not thick on the page and the sprays lack any coloured motifs. Either cost or the limner's style may be possible factors. The initial contains the arms of the Trinity (*Scutum fidei; Scutum Dei*; or *Scutum Dei triangulum*; cf. BL Cotton Dom. A. viii, f. 162r; Cotton Faust. B. vi, f. 18v) surmounted by a fine large crown; the shield occurs not infrequently as a pen-drawn diagram. The usual form of the *Scutum* is altered by a cross-bar inscribed *Vera trinitas* (Hodgett and Wormald), with an inscription on the triangle '*Pater non est spiritus non est filius non est [pater]*'. The crown is interesting as an instance of the practice of placing a crown above a coat of arms, if more usually above royal arms (cf. Pls XXIX, XXXIV,

XXXVa). On this page the crown suggests the royal founding and patronage of the church by Matilda, consort of Henry I.

Two types of important motif are present on the bar-frame: (i) the deeply scrolled and twisted acanthus (in a single colour) with a spine of dots and circles; and (ii) the bulbous flowers at the R. and lower mid-points of the bar-frame. The twisted acanthus began to be used *c.* 1410 (see Pl. VIII), and here it is evidence of at least a fifteen-year popularity. Although this acanthus was normally employed as a starting point for sprays with coloured motifs, the limner here used it to launch short sprigs of only feathering and gold motifs. The fantastic bulbous motifs with two levels of fluttering acanthus are early versions of motifs that came into wider use later in the century (cf. Pl. XVIIb, initial; Pl. XVIII). Here they are startling in the context of a bare bar-frame and of brief uncoloured sprigs. The gold balls with four pen squiggles floating apart from the bar-frame were first drawn earlier in the century, and look somewhat out of date at this time.

Colouring is modest in range, mainly blue and pink, with some use of orange. The blue is finely shaded.

This border is a mix of the past and present. The limner uses older motifs, i.e. single leaves on the bar-frame, a grouping of three leaves (L. mid-point), and 'floating' gold balls, and combines them with motifs that were recently new, i.e. deeply curled acanthus leaves at corners and large bulbous flower forms.

Plate XII *Cartularium Prioratus Sanctae Trinitatis infra Aldgate*

Cambridge, University Library, MS Ff.3.27. Ff. 1r–45r, John Sharpe, *Abbreviacio quodlibetorum Duns Scoti*; etc.

Date: 1429, Oxford: f. 45r, '. . . Scriptus fuit liber iste Anno domini M°. C°C°C°C° xx° ix°. in Oxonia'.

Description: parchment; 352 ff.; (ff. 1r–45r:) 30.9 × 21.8 cm. Red and blue paraphs. 4-line blue letters with red flourishing. One border, f. 1r.

Border: f. 1r. Although Oxford was in future decades to be in border art ahead of London in introducing new motifs, in this border the limner lags behind changes in metropolitan styles. The border has no trace of the fluidity and new motifs of, for instance, the Arundel 38 border (Pl. VIII); and it is rigid in the manner of Harley 401 (Pl. IIIb) and Fairfax 2 (Pl. VII). Only in its ample use of green does it appear abreast of the limning times. In most respects the border harks back to the beginning of the century or even to the last decade of the 14th century. The rounded, trefoil leaves with a shaded circle in white are twenty to thirty years old, as are the small roundels of leaves on the bar-frame. Other old-fashioned elements are the spray at bottom whose main support is an extended, pointed leaf rather than feathering (cf. Pl. XIV), the grouping of three leaves in the lower part of the initial (found in later 14th-century infillings and borderwork), and vines that begin inside the bar-frame. The lack of green tint on lobes of feathering is also old-fashioned for this date, but the minute size of the lobes may have affected the choice to apply or not apply green. The sprig at the end of the upper bar is unusual but no more so than a bar rather than a spray opposite the spray in the lower border (cf. Pls VIII, XIV, XX, etc.). The two deeply folded leaves in the upper part of the initial are a newer innovation, of about 1410.

The colouring of the initial is abnormally divided between orange and green and abnormally with yellow rather than white markings. The gold balls with a single rather than three squiggles are appropriate to the latter part of the 1420s.

This border, while certainly owing much to an earlier training period of the limner of some twenty to twenty-five years (and perhaps to the influence of his master) gives some indication of the state of limning activity in at least one Oxford shop before the burst of activity and innovation in the 1430s, 1440s, 1450s, and 1460s. The border also suggests how long a design might be kept in use (cf. Pls Ia, IV, origin of vines) and how long an artist might be employed, here seemingly for twenty to thirty years.

Plate XIII John Sharpe, *Abbreviacio quodlibetorum Duns Scoti* 53

Oxford, Bodleian Library, MS Bodley 795 (*SC* 2644). Ff. v–vii verso, Index; ff. 1r–244v, William Holme, *De simplicibus medicinis*; etc.

Date: 1435, Oxford, wr. by William Bedmistre: f. 244v, 'Hunc librum scripsit Willelmus Bedmistre oxonie Anno domini. 1435. Orate specialiter per eo in spicientes prefatum librum.'

Description: parchment; 314 ff.; 25 × 19 cm. In red: paraffs, underlining, strokes on capitals. One border, f. 1r.

Border: f. 1r. The large initial from which the border develops is an elongated I in pink on an engrailed gold ground laid outside of the text space [only partially visible]. I is the only letter to occur outside of the written space in 15th-century English page design; but it is more frequently laid into a triangular space, part in and part out of the text space, and may also occasionally be placed entirely within the space (Pl. Ib) like other letters of the alphabet. The initial ends in an elongated acanthus leaf whose tip is the starting point for spraywork without a bar frame. The sprays consist of regularly waving and curling feathering with circular lobes tinted in bright green, gold balls with one or three tinted squiggles, and small coloured curled leaves, all of which encloses in nearly full circles of feathering a larger coloured motif. The same motif is in each circle of feathering: an aroid flower with a longish, worm-like center and with a sort of calyx of four sepals in blue, pink, or green (see arrow). Each spray ends in a turned single leaf, green above and blue below. This single-leaf ending motif becomes more or less standard in three-sided borders of the later 1430s and the 1440s. The pink colouring here is more dampened or muted than usual, and, in a most unusual fashion, the designs on the orange aroid centers appear to be marked with silver rather than with yellow.

The scheme of a regular placement of motifs within circles or semi-circles of feathering appears here, at least, for the first time and continues in use with more or less formality into the first quarter of the 16th century (cf. Pls XXIa, XXIIIb, XXV, XXXVIIa, lower margin; and the Luton Guild Register, f. 44r: 1512). The Bodleian border is useful as an example of the spread of the elongated aroid from the first dated instance known in 1421/2 (Pl. X) until the time when it is less found, after *c.* 1455. The use of aroids, by no means only in this elongated form, becomes typical of Oxford work in the 1440s and 1450s, as does the very rounded form of lobe in the feathering. It is however perhaps indicative of a regional center that the limner had by this date not begun to use lobes on gold balls rather than squiggles with a trailing line.

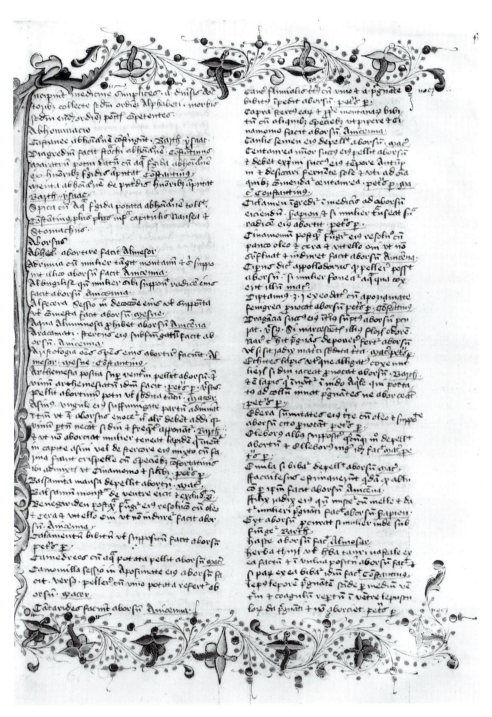

London, British Library, Royal MS 5. F.
II. Ff. 1r–91v, Athanasius, [theological
treatises], incl. ff. 1r–31v, *De humanitate verbi contra gentes*, Bk. I; ff. 32r–
66v, idem, Bk. II; ff. 66v–68v, idem, Bk.
III; ff. 70r–91r, *De unitate substantiae
deitatis dialogus*; etc. For Humfrey,
duke of Gloucester.

Datable: 1439 (Beccarria became Duke
Humfrey's secretary) – not after February 1443/4 (given to Oxford University),
wr. ?Oxford, by Antonio Beccaria of
Verona: [ff. 69v, 91v, 131v, inscrip-
tions].

Description: parchment; i + 131 + i ff.;
23.5 × 17 cm. Three 4-line spray-type
initials with grotesques, ff. 1r, 66v, 70r.
One historiated border, f. 32r (grotesques).

Border: f. 32r. This one-sided border
stands in striking contrast to the majority of other borders entered in English
books at this period. There are no
sprays, feathering, or sprigs outside the
ground of the border, and the broad
band of the ground is finished with an
irregular engrailed edge quite unlike the
usual straight sides of the English bar-
frame. Though irregular in outline, this
border still gives a controlled impression, more emphasising the first word of
each textual line rather than creating a
decorative frame for the entire text
space. The borders in this book are either by an English artist imitating Italian designs or actually by an Italian artist, like the scribe, working in England.
The breadth of ground and the many
types of grotesques are not English in
design, and there is no hint of English

Plate XVa Athanasius, *De humanitate verbi contra gentes*, Bk. II,
one-sided border

work in this or in most of the other borders, apart from the first, which, while in the same Italianate style, has sprays with feathering and gold balls that would, apart from one motif, suggest English work.

The grotesque motifs worked in and around vines include three instances of a characteristic bird-head with brushed-back feathers and a pointed beak; a bizarre hybrid with a cloven hooves, an elongated body, and a bearded male head, brandishing a scimitar; three animal heads with open mouths; a grotesque male head with long nose; and a hybrid with a bearded male head and female head in horned headdress on its rear end. The ground is coloured in amorphous shapes of rose, blue, and gold, and the colours marked with groups of three dots.

F. 70r. This briefer version of the border on f. 1r, here loosely called a 'spray' initial, is reproduced in order to confirm the reader's impression of this kind of design and its motifs. Like the border, it contains open-mouthed animal heads, hairy hybrids, birds' heads, and, further craziness, a bearded man in woman's headdress with spindle, and a hybrid with bird's head in mitre and with single cloven hoof. A well drawn tonsured head in profile is near the initial.

The Royal decoration is instructive for purposes of recognition and of definition of one important kind of Italianate-English style known to occur in books made in England. It is also useful as an example of a foreign style that did not take root in English shops as did certain other foreign styles (cf. Pl. XXVI).

Plate XVb Athanasius, *De unitate substantiae deitatis dialogus,*
  Italianate 'spray' initial

Oxford, Balliol College MS 28. Thomas Docking, *Super Deuteronomium*. For William Gray, bp. of Ely.

Date: 16 March 1442, prob. Oxford, wr. by Tielman Reyner[szoon], a Dutch scribe: f. 258r, 'Finitus per manus Tielmanni/filij Reyneri almani oriundi . . . in Hollan/dia. Anno domini M° cccc° xlij° in profesto sancte gertrudis'.

Description: parchment; 261 ff.; 39.7 × 26.9 cm. Catchwords in scrolls. Red and blue paraffs; a few decorated ascenders, e.g. f. 64r, devil's head; f. 109r, dog's head; and descenders, e.g. f. 13v, animal's head; male head in feathers. 4-line blue letters with red flourishing. One border with historiated initial (coat of arms), f. 5r.

Border: f. 5r. Although this manuscript was written by a continental scribe, the decoration can nevertheless be attributed to Oxford because the patron, Gray, was then Chancellor of the University. The border has the usual English structure of a bar frame, here with a central bar between the text columns, as well as English spraywork. The coloured motifs in sprays are overwhelmingly aroids supported by four sepals; they are used in the feathering with a few single and trefoil leaves. The border demonstrates the Oxford liking for the aroid motif, appearing as it does, in sprays, at midpoints on the bar, and in corner roundels. These aroids mainly have a flattened centre but there are also two worm-like centres as in the Oxford border of 1435 (Pl. XIV). The range of colouring is confined to green, blue, and a pale tan-rose, and the general impression of the colouring is different from the more brilliant blue, green, rose, and orange normally in use at this time. The colouring of the lobes of the feathering, normally a bright green, is here a mix of pale green, blue with white dot, and pale rose. The amount of decoration on the page and in sprays is right for the period.

Compared to earlier borders (cf. Pls XII, XIII), there is more use of elongated leaves on the corner roundels, on the central and vertical bars, and in the area on two sides of the initial. One of the vine roundels by the initial contains a spiky monochrome acanthus leaf found in earlier manuscripts (cf. Pl. VIII). The arms of Gray, donor of the book to Balliol, are in the initial, a site often used for ownership signs.

On the whole, the border is a fusion of conventional English elements (design, spraywork, leaf motifs, initial) with elements that are probably characteristic of Oxford (two kinds of aroid) and of the artist (colouring). The border may be an early dated instance of the large-scale use of aroids in Oxford limning shops, an interest that may afterwards have become more general in England until about 1470.

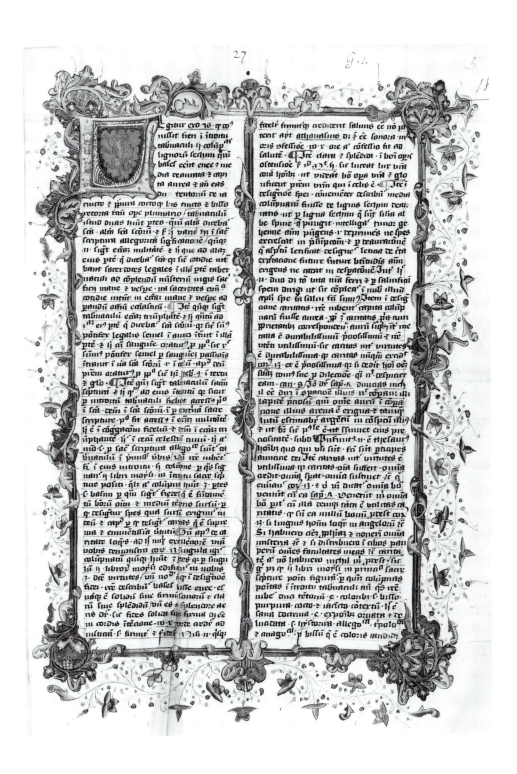

Plate XVI Thomas Docking, *Super Deuteronomium*,
bar border with mid-column bar

1440 – before Feb. 1444, ? King's Lynn

Plates XVIIa–b

Oxford, Bodleian Library, MS Duke Humfrey b.1 (*S.C.* 32386). John Capgrave, *Commentarius in Exodum*. For Humfrey, duke of Gloucester.

Datable: after May 1440 (date of composition) and not after 1444 (date of donation by Humfrey to Oxford University), revised by Capgrave, ?Kings's Lynn, Norfolk: f. 186r: [inscription concerning dates of composition].

Description: parchment; 183 ff.; 40.8 × 26.5 cm. Catchwords in shaded scrolls. In red: underlining, stroking on capitals. 1-line blue capitals; 5-line blue letters with red flourishing, with f. 183v, head in chaperon and speech scroll. Two borders, ff. 3r, 3v; one historiated initial, f. 3r (Capgrave presenting book to Duke Humfrey); column miniatures, unframed, ff. 114r (2x), 118v (2x), 122r, 125r, 126r, 127r (2x), 130r, 133v.

Border: f. 3r. The first impression of this introductory border is the density of motif, with spraywork that is virtually impenetrable. The motifs across the top consist of twisted and turned acanthus leaves, two large aroids with a leafy calyx, smaller leaves, and a smaller aroid. The motifs in the lower spray are similar. Most of the aroids are unusually large for this date and probably a recent fashion. The bar frame at the side has an aroid flower at the mid-point between the initial and lower roundel, as is customary in the 1440s.

This border offers a clear instance of what were probably standard proportions in width between top, side, and lower borders, with the lower border being the most important. Whether the lines remain or not, it is also apparent that borders might by this time be ruled and kept to a clearly delimited space, although oddly here extending beyond the written space. The range of colour is rose, blue, green and orange, used in more or less equal proportions, the blue less bright than usual. Given the high quality of the historiated initial and given the difference in style between this and the next border, it is questionable whether the same artist made both borders.

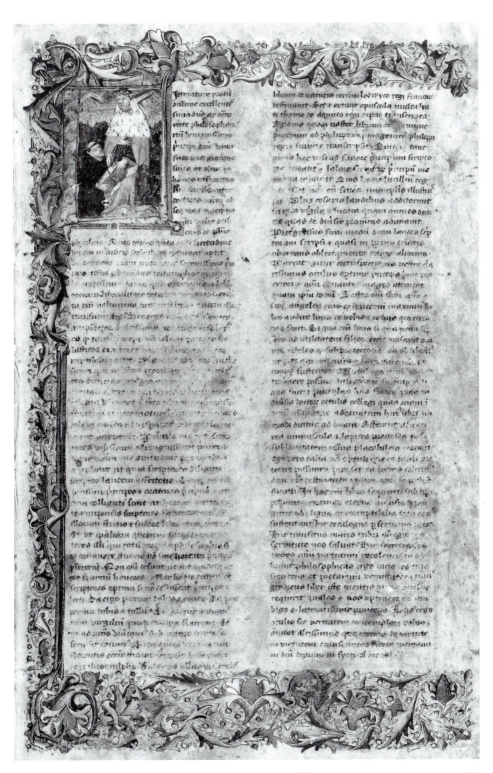

Plate XVIIa John Capgrave, *Commentarius in Exodum*,
    introductory page, three-sided bar and spraywork border

F. 3v. The second border, back to back with the first, seems to come from a different world from the first, with motifs unusual for the period: profile daisy buds (top); trefoil- and quatrefoil trumpets; and residual interlaces at the midpoint and bottom of the bar. These motifs had been out of style for 15 to 20 years, and, in the case of the interlace, even longer. Other unusual motifs are the pointed leaves in the lower spray and the gold balls turned into flower forms by drawing them with five or six pen lobes/petals. These two motifs are almost certainly regional traits, that is, of Eastern England (incl. Cambridgeshire, Lincoln, Norfolk but not Bury St Edmunds) by connection with other manuscripts in which the daisy-ball appears. None of these motifs appear in the first border, but the acanthus leaves are similar enough in colouring and rendering that, although the borders are very different in design and motif, they may be by the same regional artist, who, like a scribe and his scripts, was able to produce a different hierarchy of borders for different positions in the text.

London, Public Record Office E 164/10.
Ff. 2r–312v, *Nova statuta Angliae*, 1
Ed. III–23 Hen. VI (Fr.); ff. 313r–335r,
continuations to 39 Hen. VI.

Datable: shortly after 23 Hen. VI = *c.*
1445/6, prob. London.

Description: parchment; 352 ff.; 27.2 ×
18.2 cm. Red and blue paraphs. 3-line
blue and gold letters with red and blue
flourishing; 4-line gold letters on rose/
blue ground with brief sprays; 4- or 5-
line blue letters with red flourishing, alternating with gold letters with brown
flourishing. Five borders, ff. 44r, 124v,
183r, 217v, and 241r.

Border: f. 44r. This border is a fine example of the prevalent English style of
the mid-century. The design is in proportion with the text space, and the corner motifs with the spraywork. Each
area of spraywork between acanthus
clusters contains a different type of coloured motif from the others, usually a
sign of quality in a border: (lower L.)
two trumpet flowers and a cup; (lower
R.) three rounded aroids with three sepals; (R. lower) two bell-like flowers
with four pointed sepals; and (R. upper)
six trumpet flowers with lobed and
back-turned petals. Acanthus leaves at
the four corners are sinuously drawn,
some with white striations, a new mode
of giving dimension to a motif; see also
the petals of the large lower aroid. All of

the sprays, with or without coloured motifs, contain spiky gold trefoils and pine
cones, as well as gold balls with green
lobes, the three preferred gold motifs at
this time.

Larger aroids are also a part of the
vocabulary at two of the more important sites of decoration on the bar-frame.
The ten-line initial contains a fine aroid
flower whose lower bulbous centre is
enclosed in a spathe of deeply lobed and
curled leaves while the long, thin apex
of the spadix projects above the letter.
Another less elaborate aroid hangs from
the lower mid-point of the bar-frame.
The pairs of curved lines and rows of
dots on the spadix are a common design
for this kind of growth, especially as
here, coloured in orange with yellow
designs. Otherwise the colours of painted motifs, as usual for the period, are
blue, rose, and green, with scattered use
of orange for the return of a leaf and other small motifs. The intertwined leaves
and vines at upper and lower R. corners
and at the R. mid-point came into use in
this decade and continued to be used until the end of the century.

Apart from the individuality of the
artist as expressed in the initial aroid
and in the bell- and trumpet-like motifs
in the R. vertical spraywork, this border
is at the same time conventional and
representative of first-rate London work
in the favoured style at this period.

Plate XVIII *Nova statuta Angliae*   65

Oxford, Bodleian Library, MS Bodley 362 (*S.C.* 2463). Ff. 1r–247v, John of Gaddesden, *Rosa medicinae (Rosa Anglica)*; ff. 248r–272r, Bernard Alberti, Commentary on four books of Avicenna's Canon; ff. 272v–334v, Petrus de Tossignano, *Spiritus medicinarum*; etc. For Gilbert Kymer.

Date: Seven colophons with a date, incl. f. 184r, 1448; ff. 185r, 237v, 246v, 1449/50; f. 272r, 1453; and f. 334v, 1454/5 = [for borderwork] 1448–January 1455, but possibly *c.* 1455, wr. by Hermann Zurke, of Greifswold.

Description: parchment; 337 ff.; 33.4 × 22.5 cm. In red: underlining. Red and blue paraffs. Calligraphic letters, sometimes with profile heads. 2-, 4-, 5-, and 7-line blue letters with red flourishing. Two spray borders, ff. 248r, 272v; one bar-frame border, f. 1r.

Border: f. 1r. If the previous border (Pl. XVIII) is very good standard English work, this border, while recognizably English, is an extreme provincial deviation from the standard. The coloured motifs in the sprays are *sui generis*, the feathering has no green tint on the lobes, and the introductory initial is drastically out of proportion to the text space compared with most other border pages of this period, that is, the initial is 18 lines high, more than a third the height of the written lines. The motifs in the sprays are limited to two kinds: kidney and trefoil leaves. The kidneys are more circular than kidney-shaped and the trefoils, unlike others made in English shops, are composed of three circular shapes placed together. Both kinds stand out from the feathering because of the lack of green tint. The gold balls, instead of the usual three lobes or squiggles, show five or six curled pen lines. A rounded aroid (with folded acanthus leaves) appears in the initial, at mid-points on three bars, at three corners, and at each end of the initial base. The aroid was very commonly used in Oxford illuminating shops at this period, but this border artist has not been recognized in a manuscript certainly written in Oxford. He apparently had knowledge of some of the currently favoured motifs, to judge from his placing of aroids in the most important positions on the border. His colour range of pink, blue, orange, and green for motifs is standard for the period, and his use of roundels with folded acanthus also shows knowledge of designs from previous decades. The other two spray borders in the book were probably made by this artist at about the same time as the full border.

The scribe states on f. 272r that he was writing in Salisbury, but the *Summary Catalogue* notes that the earlier parts of the manuscript may have been written in Oxford in that they were done for Gilbert Kymer, Chancellor of Oxford, from 1448 to May 1553. All in all, however, the rendering would suggest that the artist was not employed in a major illuminating centre and that the attribution of the writing of a later part of the manuscript to Salisbury would also indicate the site of limning.

Plate XIX John of Gaddesden, *Rosa medicinae*, full bar border

Cambridge, University Library, MS Ee.5.21. Ff. 5r–10v, Calendar; ff. 11r–27v, Table of Contents; ff. 29r–127r, *Registrum statutorum ecclesie et consuetudinum cathedralis sancti Pauli londoniarum*; etc.

Date: 1450, prob. London (on grounds of destination): f. 28v, 'Anno henrici Regis anglie post conquestum sexti .xxixº'.

Description: parchment; 151 ff.; 28.9 × 20.4 cm. Red and blue paraphs. In red: underlining, titles, chapter numbers. 2- and 4- line blue letters with red flourishing. One border, f. 29r.

Border: f. 29r. The distinction of this border is that it has few distinctive traits and is nevertheless a good if scanty base from which to judge London styles around 1450. The colour range is conventional: rose/pink, blue, green, with minor use of a dusky orange. The initial S is backfilled with leaves in those colours and with vines that develop from the initial ends. The letter is halved rose/blue with crisp indentations and cross-hatching and, below them, a row of dots with a single circle that is also conventional. The vine in a curlicue at the L. top of the letter is a new motif that comes into use in London, whereas the green pen squiggles along the side of the initial and bar-frame are common motifs.

Sprays in the upper and lower margins are often introduced at the end of the bar at this period by two leaves whose stems are intertwined. The feathering of the two sprays is in black ink with lobes tinted green. Near the end of each spray a branch of feathering curls back on itself, partly enclosing a coloured leaf. The green lobes on gold balls are more elongated than usual and surmounted by a pen squiggle, an unusual double elaboration of the gold ball motif. In the lower margin the coloured motifs are all single leaves and, apart from one, not curled; they are not distinctive. In the upper spray there are two trumpet motifs with stamens. Each spray ends with a nondescript single leaf, a theme also typical of this period and earlier (cf. Pl. XIV).

Although the border shows a few minor and unavoidable personal traits of the artist (rendering of gold balls), the border is both typical of London and a second example (see also Pl. XVIII) of a style that will persist for about four decades, if not reproduced in this handbook with the same frequency as it occurs in manuscripts.

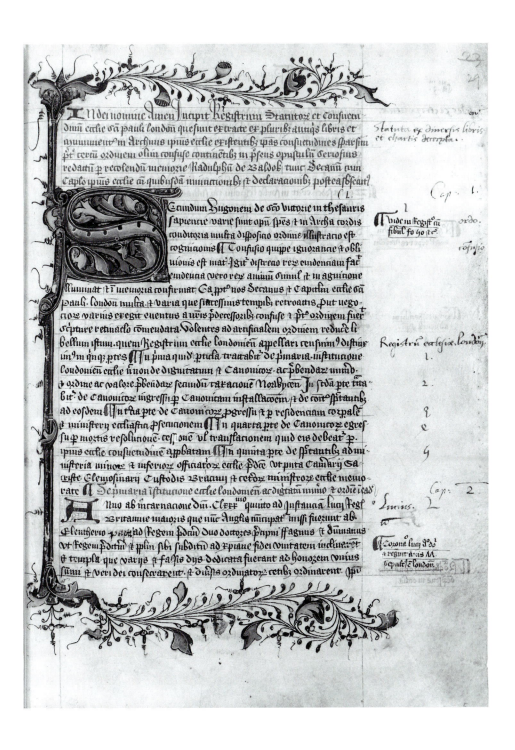

In dei nomine Amen Incipit Registrum Statutorum et consuetud[inum] d[omi]n[or]um eccl[es]ie s[an]c[t]i pauli london que sunt extracte ex pluribus antiquis libris et munimentis in Archivis ip[s]ius eccl[es]ie existentib[us]; ip[s]as consuetudines sparsim pr[ius] p[er] cert[um] ordinem olim confuse contentib[us]; in p[rese]ns opusculu[m] seriosius redacti[s] p[er] recolend[um] memorie Radulphum de Baldok tunc Decan[um] cum Cap[itu]lo ip[s]ius eccl[es]ie cu[m] quibusd[am] munitionib[us]; [e]t declaracionib[us]; postea sub scan[...]

Statuta ex diuersis libris; et chartis deterpta.

C.I.

Cap. I.

Secundum Hugonem de s[an]c[t]o victore in thesauris sapientie varie sunt op[er]um sp[eci]es [e]t in Archa cordis conditoria mu[l]tra disposicio ordin[e] illustracio est cognicio[n]is ¶ Confusio quippe ignorancie [e]t obli uionis est mat[er] Igit[ur] distrecio rex euidencia[m] fac euidencia vero rex a[n]imu[m] s[i]m[u]l [e]t in agnicione illuminat [e]t memoria confirmat Ca[usa] p[ro]pt[er] nos Decanus [e]t Capit[u]lu[m] eccl[es]ie s[an]c[t]i pauli. london mu[l]ta [e]t varia que s[uccess]iuis tempib[us] retroactis p[ro]ut nego cior[um] varijs exe[g]it euentus a ur[...] p[re]decessorib[us] confuse [e]t p[re]t[er] ordinem fuer[unt] scripture b[...] comendata Volentes ad arti[ficio]salem ordinem reduce[re] li bellum istum quem Registrum eccl[es]ie londonien[sis] appellari censuim[us] distur im[...] m[...] pt[e]s ¶ In p[ri]ma quid[em] p[re]s[en]s tractabit de p[ri]maria institucione Londonien[sis] eccl[es]ie [e]t no[n] de dignitatum [e]t Canonicor[um]· ac p[re]bendar[um] numb. [e]t ordine ac valore p[re]bendar[um] secundu[m] taxacionem No[rwa]kpen In s[ecun]da p[ar]te trac bit· de Canonicor[um] ingressu p[er] Canonicam installacoem [e]t de eor[um] s[ib]i aunib[us] ad eosdem ¶ In t[er]cia p[ar]te de Canonicor[um] p[ro]gressu [e]t p[er] residenciam corpale[m] [e]t ministerij eccl[es]iastic[i] p[ro]secucionem ¶ In quarta p[ar]te de Canonicor[um] egres su p[er] mortis resolucione· cess[ati]one vel translacionem quid eis debeat[ur] p[...] ip[s]ius eccl[es]ie consuetudine[m] app[ro]batam ¶ In quinta p[ar]te de p[re]s[en]tib[us]; ad mi[n]isteria minora [e]t inferiora officiatora[um] eccl[es]ie p[...] v[e]t p[ut]a Cam[er]arij Sa criste Elemosinarij Custodis Brac[...] [e]t ceor[um] ministror[um] eccl[es]ie memo rare ¶ De p[ri]maria institucione eccl[es]ie londonien[sis] ac dignitatum numo [e]t ordie[...] ead[...]

Anno ab incarnacione d[omi]ni Clerc[...] quinto ad Instancia[m] Lucij Reg[is] Britanie maioris que nunc Anglia nuncipat[ur] missi fuerunt ab Eleutherio p[a]p[a] ad Regem p[re]d[ictu]m duo doctores p[re]dic[tores] ffag[n]us [e]t Duuianus v[e]t Regem p[re]d[ictu]m [e]t ip[su]m s[ib]i subdit[um] ad xpiane fidei v[er]itatem incline[...]t [e]t templa que varijs [e]t falsis dijs dedicata fuerant ad honore[m] vnius s[um]mi [e]t veri dei consecrarent [e]t diuisis ordinator[um] cetib[us] ordinarent· p[...]

Unde in Regist[ro] an[tiquo] sib[us] fo 40 [e]c[etera]

ordo.

[con]f[u]sio

Registru[m] eccl[es]ie londoni[ensis]
I.
2.
3.
4.
5.

Cap. 2

Lucius.

¶ Corona[ti]o[n] lucij p[r]o[n]o [e]t regnu[m] a[nn]is M. s[ub] pa[...] p[...]e londo[n]

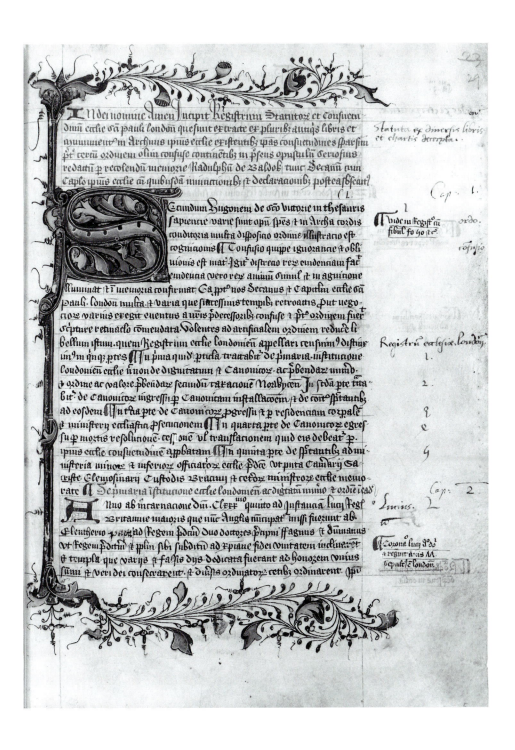

In dei nomine Amen Incipit Registrum Statutorum et consuetud[inum]...

Plate XX *Registrum statutorum ecclesie et consuetudinum cathedralis sancti Pauli,* three-sided border

69

1453; 1455; 1456; 1459, ?Salisbury

Oxford, Bodleian Library, MS Bodley 361 (*S.C.* 2462). Medical miscellany, incl. pp. 1–111, Stephen Arnald, *Dietarium*; pp. 113–203, Bartholomaeus Salernitanus, *Practica medicine*; pp. 203–330, Johannes de Sancto Paulo [Platearius], inc. 'Assiduis peticionibus me karissimi compendiose morborum signa;' etc. Possibly for Gilbert Kymer.

Dates: p. 111, 30 May 1459; p. 203, 15 October 1455, in Salisbury ('in villa Sarum'; Pl. XXIb)); p. 330, 16 October 1456; p. 334, 20 October 1456; p. 393, 6 November 1453; p. 424, 28 November 1453 ('Sarum ciuitate'); p. 458, 14 December 1453 ('in ciuitate Sarum'), wr. by Hermann Zurke [of Greifswold].

Description: parchment; 508 pp.; 33.4 × 22.5 cm. Red and blue paraffs. In red: underlining. 2-, 3- and 4-line blue letters with red flourishing; 5-line gold letters on quartered rose/blue ground with sprays. Three 3-sided borders, pp. 1, 113, 203.

Border: p. 1. Although this border occurs in a manuscript whose writing is localized in several parts to Salisbury, the style is of Oxford or London, and the border may not have been made by a Salisbury limner. The rest of the illuminated work (Pl. XXIb) may have been made by the limner of Bodley 362 (Pl. XIX), and since this second limner is in every part located in Salisbury, he is likely to have been a resident limner. The first border is then included to emphasize that a limner who was evidently considered the master (and who may have been the head of a shop) often made the first (and most important) border in a book (and no other) and often worked in a noticeably different style.

The first border has the usual bar-frame that develops into leaf and flower motifs, both on the bar and at top and bottom. The motifs at each end of the bar are remarkably alike, a larger aroid with spiky lobes outlined in black as the starting point for the spray and a smaller, more rounded aroid with a circular base pointing in the opposite direction towards the gutter. The sprays are also closely matched and are unusual for having exactly the same type of motif, barbed quatrefoils, in the same position in the feathering, with two ending leaves in the same position and colouring, as are the other two single leaves. The sprays appear to have been ruled to a fixed space. The mid-point between the initial and the lower corner has an aroid, and the spraywork between is filled with conventional kidneys and hearts.

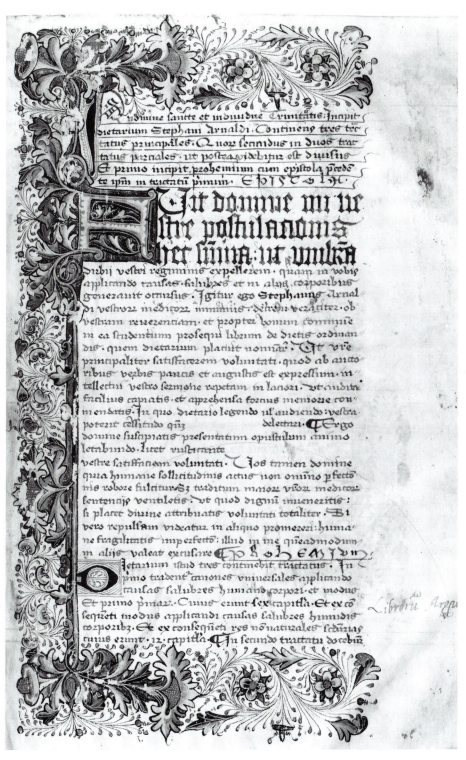

Plate XXIa Stephen Arnald, *Dietarium*, first text page, three-sided border 71

P. 203. The borders on pp. 113 and 203 were made by a third artist who reflects certain Oxford traits, such as the frequent use of aroids, even if occurring with a localization in Salisbury. The border opposite shows a relatively plain aroid in the initial, slightly elongated heart motifs, and illustionistic piercing of the gold ground by the vine that begins the sprays. The elongated hearts are probably a motif characteristic of a Salisbury limner.

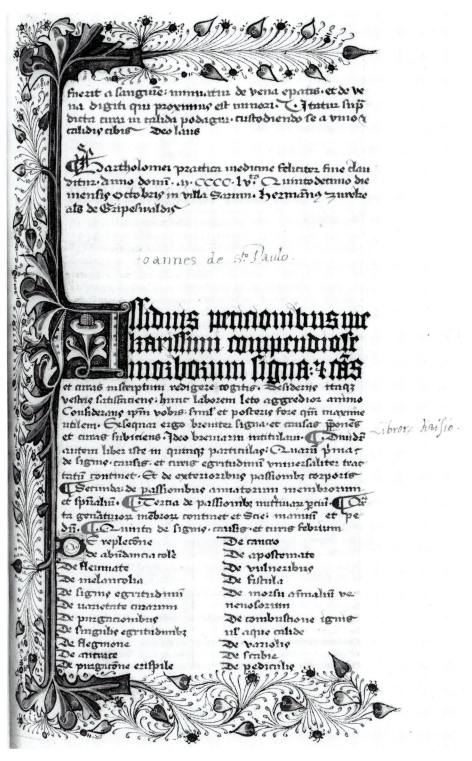

Plate XXIb Johannes de Sancto Paulo, inc. 'Assiduis peticionibus',
opening of third text, three-sided border

c. 1453, ? Eastern England
Plate XXII

Winchester, College Library, MS 13B. [Genealogical Chronicle], inc. 'Considerans cronicorum prolixitatem necnon et difficultatem scolariumque circa studium nobilis progenie regum anglie', with later continuations.

Datable: In or shortly after 1453: membr. 11, [birth of Edward IV] '. . . genuit edwardum principem qui natus erat in festo translacionis sancti edwardi regis [con]fessoris anno dm. m° cccc°. liij.' Prob. wr. London; decorated ?Eastern England.

Description: parchment; (roll) 11 membranes; 34.9 (wide) cm. Red and gold paraff signs. 1-line gold letters with flourishing in pale rose; one 4-line gold letter on rose and blue ground (at inc. 'Adam in agro'); one border with historiated vine roundels. Red roundels; lines of descent in gold, blue, red, green, and yellowy tan; roundels surmounted by a crown; (historiated roundels, membr. 1 (the Fall).

Border: membr. 1. This unusual decoration is made up of a broad band (*c.* 7 cm. high) of roundels with images, above which stretches inhabited spraywork. The border descends along the L. margin in increasingly smaller vine roundels that enclose leaves or flowers and that terminate in a pointed blue and chartreuse aroid flower. Spraywork of quatrefoils and single leaves in pale blue, green, and rose extends to the lower edge of the membrane [not visible]. The R. border also commences with a series of decreasing vine and leaf roundels that enclose small aroids or leaves, ending in a fantastic flower from which spraywork begins. The feathering work has small quatre-

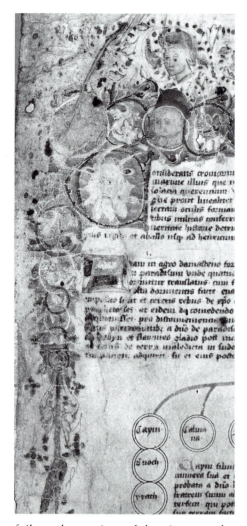

foils and prominent lobes in a murky chartreuse. The main interest of this border is the upper portion, which contains roundels (*c.* 2.3 cm.) with human and animal heads, fantastic flowers, and grotesques. The roundels read from L. to R.: (i) [much rubbed] ?a bearded head in yellow or wash gold; (ii) a curled leaf; (iii) a bearded head in a rounded red cap, with face in wash gold; (iv) two leaves; (v) red grotesque animal curled up; (vi) flower; (vii) white swan-like grotesque with curved horns; (viii) curled leaf; (ix) lion head; (x) flower; (xi) bust

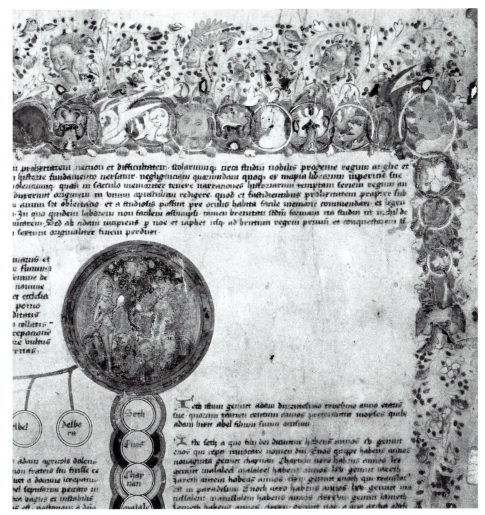

of white horse; (xii) flower; (xiii) curled leaf; (xiv) red swan-like bird; and (xv) bust of youth, in white gown. The spraywork above contains four heads: (i) young man, ?in hat; (ii) bearded man; (iii) man wearing stag's antlers; and (iv) bearded head partly bald. The initial (damaged) also contains a head, perhaps of a satyr, with horns and animal ears, emerging from a ruffled collar or flower.

Both the style and colouring of this border suggest that it was not made in London, even though the scribe is known to have worked there. The border is an early occurrence of the revitalization of borders with images. The extensive use of pale colouring, of chartreuse, and of virtual reservework images on a gold ground (as in the initial), of white for prominent images, and of small quatrefoils suggest a limner's shop in the east of England. The mix of pale colours with a strong red and white may be a characteristic of the limner. As noticeable on Pls XVIIa and XXIa, density of spraywork has become an aesthetic value by this time.

Oxford, Exeter College, MS. 62. Hugh of St Cher, *In Matthaeum et Marcum*. Arms of Roger Keys, archdeacon of Barnstaple.

Date: 1454, Oxford, wr. by William Salamon, of León: f. 179v, 'Iste liber constat Magistro Rogero/ Keys qui fuit scriptus Oxonie Anno / domini millesimo quadringentisimo / quinquagesimo quarto. Per manum Willi / Salamonis leonensis diocesis. . . .'

Description: parchment; 181 ff.; 40.8 × 27.5 cm. In red: underlining, incipits. Red and blue paraffs; blue running titles. Decorated and illustrated ascenders. 2-line gold letters on a rose/blue ground with sprays. 2 [surviving] borders, ff. 130v (with coat of arms), 132r.

Border: f. 130v. A chief characteristic of this border is its animation: the elongated leaves seem to whip about in a wind of the artist's making. The feathering is drawn in a pale brown ink, and the lobes of the feathering are in a pale green, adding to the effect of lightness and movement. The basic structure of the bar-frame is unusual in being placed only on the left and upper sides, and, exceptionally, not in the lower margin, leaving the Keys coat of arms hanging without credible support. Sprays from the upper and lower borders do not quite meet in the R. margin, where it is however not uncommon to have sprays without a bar not quite joining.

The plethora of aroid flowers (14) of various types is a characteristic of Oxford borders at this period. Here the aroids are used as single motifs floating in the sprays, as filling within a vine roundel (lower L.), as a motif outside of the roundel, and as a direct growth from the bar-frame. The spadices may be elongated, rounded, or conical; and they are coloured green with yellow or, as generally in the 15th century, orange with yellow dots or lines. The single leaves that end a spray may also be a trait of Oxford limning shops at this period. The many single leaves are coloured green, blue, and pink. Some of the orange leaf motifs (e.g. upper R. corner) have a bronze tone, a colour used in Oxford but not elsewhere. One motif is unusual and probably characteristic of this artist, that is, the gold pine cone with three coloured sepals, some cones having pen lines like bristles (lower border). As a whole, the lightness and movement of this border, the elongated single leaves with a curl at the end, and the heavy use of aroids are notable.

F. 132r. Part of the second surviving border is reproduced in order to show a series of aroids enclosed uniformly in feathering; the flat but pointed aroid is typical of this Oxford limner and found in other manuscripts decorated by him.

Plate XXIIIa Hugh of St Cher, *In Matthaeum et Marcum*,
mixed bar and spray border

77

Oxford, Bodleian Library, MS Lat. theol. b.5. Pp. 1–524, Hugh of St Cher, Commentary on Isaiah (Lat.); pp. 525–597, Johannes de Rupella, *Postille super Danielem*; pp. 601–827, anon., Commentary on the Apocalypse (Lat.).

Dates: 1456; 1455, wr. by Matthew of Moravia: p. 597, 'ffinitur per me Matheum de Morauia diocesis Olomuncensis cuius metropolis ciuitas regalis pragen. Sub anno do' Millimo CCC.lvj.'; p. 827: '... Et finitur per me Matheum de Moravia nacionis Germanorum diocesis Olomuncensis cuius metropolis Pragensis Anno grace millmio CCCC.lv. . . .'

Description: parchment; 830 pp.; 38.3 × 28.3 cm. Red underlining. 4-line blue letters with red flourishing; 8-line initials in colours on gold ground with sprays, pp. 1, 525, 601.

Border: p. 1. This initial and spraywork has been included because of its very typical style and for its continuity with the borders in the same basic style (Pls XVIII, XX, XXVIII, and XXXVIIa). This particular design hovers between a border and a spray initial (see Introduction, p. 11), and could be described as a spray initial extended to border proportions. Its position on the first text page certainly suggests that it was intended to function as a border. The initial contains a vine and curled leaves (coloured in rose, blue, and green) that develop on a diagonal across the interior space. The vines continue from letter-ends outside of the burnished gold base to develop acanthus leaves and an aroid flower with an orange dotted spadix. The leaves at R. just above the initial are multilobed and scarcely curled, while the leaves at L. are twisted or curled, with a backward-facing flower. The reverse of the flower is striated in white, a type of marking characteristic of the second half of the century.

The feathering of the two sprays develops at the end of the initial base from a leaf and from the reversed flower. The feathering is a loose open wave supporting tighter curls that enclose curled leaves. Each spray ends with a single, straight leaf, and it is important to note the occurrence together of both straight and curled leafs in the third quarter of the century. The gold motifs in the feathering are pine cones with prickles in black ink and balls with three squiggles tinted green. Each margin side of the initial has two sprigs of green feathering and gold pine cones.

It is possible to say that every motif and colour is typical of the third quarter of the 15th century, and that the design without a bar-frame and limited to two margins is also not uncommon. The spray borders on pp. 525 and 601 of the manuscript contain another common motif in the period, a heart-shaped leaf, which is in both cases the only coloured motif used in the feathering

Plate XXIV Hugh of St Cher, Commentary on Isaiah, spraywork border   79

London, Lambeth Palace Library, MS 15 (**printed book**). 42-line Bible (New Testament only).

Datable: *c.* 1455 (printed in Mainz before 15 August 1455).

Description: parchment; i + 128 ff.; 45.5 × 29 cm. In red: running titles, chapter numbers, incipits, explicits. 1-line blue letters; 2-line blue letters with red flourishing; 4- or 5-line gold letters on coloured ground with brief sprays; 5-line coloured letters on a gold ground with sprays. 27 borders.

Border: f. 18r. Apart from its association with the earliest printing in Europe, this book is of considerable interest for both its mode of production and its decoration. The borders were produced in a country different from that of the text, a not unparalled circumstance; there is an example of another English border in the fragment of a second 42-line Bible (BL, IC.5ba, [DD] 7 recto), although not by the same limner (Koenig, fig. 1). The differentiation of Jerome prologues by sprays (see Pl. XXV, L. col.) and initials shows, like the numerous borders, the considerable care and expense taken with the book. Of further exceptional interest is the survival of letters and signs made in red in margins as indications to the illuminator of the type of decoration to be entered (see arrow). On f. 1v, c and an abbreviation sign indicate the limner's term *champ*; on ff. 18r, 60v, 77r, 79r, and 86r, the three-sided border is indicated by an **h** (meaning unknown) in red (Pl. XXV); and on several other folios (83r, 88v, 90r) a red dot near the initial seems to have served the same function. These letters were entered opposite the large initial, in this plate in the R. margin (faint) opposite the letter **I** of the column border. The borders were probably added not long after the accepted date of printing of *c.* 1455. The English style of the borders is not necessarily that of London; and whether the importer or the buyer commissioned the decoration is merely speculation. The spraywork shows one type of regularization of motifs that had begun to happen as early as the 1430s (Pl. XIV) but that became common in the second half of the century: continuous and rhythmic curvilinear spaces formed by feathering, enclosing a single coloured motif (here, a single leaf). The ink of the spraywork in this book is usually pale and enhances the regular placement of the leaf motifs. Interspersed in the sprays are spiky gold trefoils and pine cones, the latter a sign of the second half of the century. An aroid, a favorite motif of this and the previous two decades, appears at the top and upper part of the mid-bar. The colouring of motifs is less brilliant than usual at this time and may be a characteristic of the artist rather than the period, as may be the limited selection of coloured motifs (mainly leaves).

Aspects of the Lambeth borders new in the early 1450s are: cross-hatching on some leaf motifs and an initial design with a vine that starts at one corner of the letter and sweeps upwards diagonally with leaves filling the interior space (see also Pls XXIIIa, XXIV).

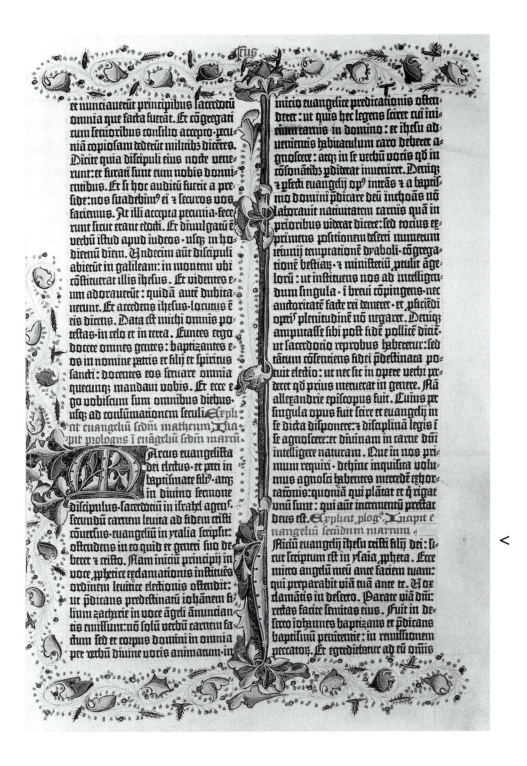

Plate XXV 42-line Bible, prologue to Mark,
column border and spray initial

Oxford, Balliol College MS 204. John Duns Scotus, *Ordinatio IV*. Coat of arms of William Gray, Bp. of Ely.

Date: Finished 17 March 1461; wr. Johannes Reynbold, from Zierenberg, Hesse: f. 279r, 'Explicit . . . . Scriptum per me Johannem Reyn/boldi Almanicum de Monte ornato terre Hassie. Anno domini Mil/lesimo. CCCC^{mo} sexagesimo primo decimoseptimo die mensis Marcij.'

Description: parchment; 281 ff.; 43.5 × 30 cm. In red and blue: running titles, paraphs. 3- and 6-line blue letters in non-English style with red flourishing. One border with historiated initial (coat of arms), f. 1r.

Border: f. 1r. As is at once obvious, this two-sided border was not made by an artist trained in the English tradition, and his proficiency suggests that he was actually trained in a continental shop. The border is enclosed by ruled lines that occur on every page in the manuscript, perhaps made as guides for titles and glosses, and the internal structure of the border is based on black pen lines that coil through the space. These pen lines are mainly decorated with short uncoloured squiggles, giving the impression of light, open work. The coloured motifs are, at L., single strawberries and strawberry leaves and, at top, poppy-head motifs and pink and blue flowers. The smaller motifs in both sprays are gold-based: balls, trefoils, clasps, caterpillar-like motifs, pine cones, and blue triangles with a gold ball on each side. The sparse effect of these sprays is counterpoised by a large introductory initial with Gray's arms and by a large branch of roses and leaves with a smaller branch of barbed blue quatrefoils below. The roses and their ciliate leaves are rendered in a naturalistic manner, and this is the earliest known dated instance of this use of roses in an English book. The rose theme may have entered England through this limner and through Oxford, but caution is needed as other, undated manuscripts, perhaps made in London, may also have been a source of these motifs, more or less simultaneously (Introduction, pp. 12-13). The position of the branch beside the initial occasionally occurs elsewhere but it is more commonly placed within the border between corners and mid-points, or at corners (Pls XXXII, XXXVb).

The initial is in a foreign style that was taken up and used in English manuscripts. The letter is blue with white markings in a non-English design and is laid on a burnished gold base with engrailed edges; the letter is infilled with unusually brightly coloured acanthus that can be even more prominent in other initials of this type.

This artist or his immediate followers (see Scott, *Survey*, no. 123, ills. 448–450) worked in a considerable number of other manuscripts made in England, and, although his work is wholly foreign in style and rendering, it is important to be aware of this work and of the copying of his work by native limners (cf. Harvard Univ. Law School 25; Bristol City Reference Library MS 9; Glasgow UL Hunterian 5 (S.1.5), ff. 124v, 138r, with an English artist, e.g. f. 18v).

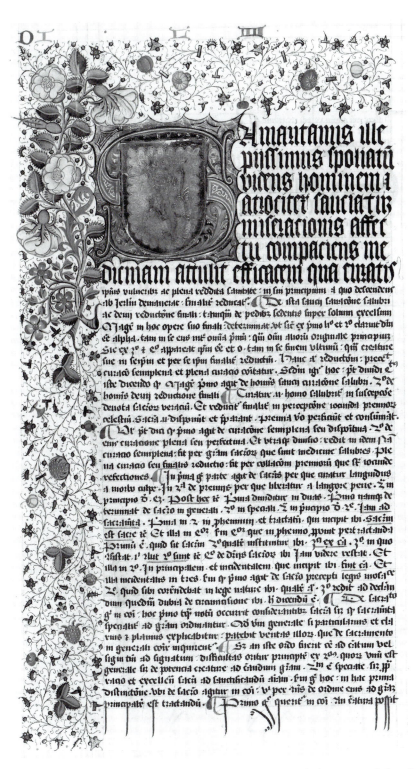

Plate XXVI John Duns Scotus, *Ordinatio IV*, two-sided spraywork border 83

Oxford, Bodleian Library, MS Bodley 108 (*S.C.* 1960). Ff. 1r–63v, John Bury, *Gladius Salomonis*, Bk I (Lat. and Eng.), with preface addressed to Thomas Bourchier, Archbishop of Canterbury, 1454–?1486.

Datable: *c.* 1457 (written) – prob. not after 1461 (see below).

Description: parchment; 64 ff.; 24.5 × 17.3 cm. Red and blue paraffs. 2-line blue letters with red flourishing; one 2-line gold letter on rose/blue ground, with sprays, f. 3v; one 4- and one 6-line coloured letter on gold, with border sprays, ff. 1r, 3r.

Border: f. 1r. This manuscript has by exception a border at both the (Latin) preface (f. 1r) and the beginning of the text in English (f. 3r). Since the borders are much alike in structure and motif, the first one with a larger and slightly more elaborate initial is reproduced. Although only two-sided, the borders and spray initial on f. 3v are of significance because they were made by a limner whose decoration has been identified in manuscripts almost certainly made in Eastern England, probably Suffolk. Two of these related books (Bodl. Lib. Rawl. liturg.f.2; New York, Pierpont Morgan M 124) have arms of East Anglian families; and others have a Bury St Edmunds (Rawl. liturg.e.42) or Norwich use (Rawl. C.560) or feasts (Trinity College, Cambridge, MS O.5.3). Others with borders by the hand of the Bodley-108 limner (BL Yates Thompson 47; Arundel Castle; and Bodl. Lib. Ashmole 47) are all copies of John Lydgate's Lives of SS. Edmund and Fremund, both East Anglian saints, datable after 1461 and the accession of Ed. IV. We could wish for a more satisfying attribution of time and place but must risk these attributions in order to assure that the style, certainly East Anglian, is recognized. Because Bodley 108 suggests a modest presentation copy, it is possibly datable more precisely to 'shortly after 1457'; it is also relevant that the text inveighs against Reginald Pecock, who was condemned *c.* 1458 and died in 1460 or 1461. Bury's book was not likely to be copied after Pecock's death.

The borders are of a distinctive colouring, using blue and green, with a muted pink and orange. As usual with this limner, the sprays begin from a pointed aroid centre, whose petals are in either pink and deeper pink or in blue and deeper blue. Pairs of kidney and curled leaves are also normal for this hand, as is the concluding motif of the spray of either a rounded aroid or an extended single leaf. The feathering is usually in a shade of brown; and the floating gold balls (cf. f. 3r) often have long finishing strokes (cf. MS. O.5.3).

Plate XXVIIa John Bury, *Gladius Salomonis*, first page of Introduction, spraywork border

F. 3v. The design of the spraywork here is also typical of this limner at *c.* 1460, as well as of East Anglian decoration of an earlier date (cf. BL Add. 11814, 1445, Clare, Suffolk, where John Bury was an Austin friar). The initial is of a champ type with the letter, ground and sprays conforming to type. The spray is lengthened, however, nearly to the size of a two-sided border. Finally, note (in the original) the use of a pale fuzzy green tint on pen squiggles and gold motifs. The long finishing strokes in pen and ink are also typical of this style.

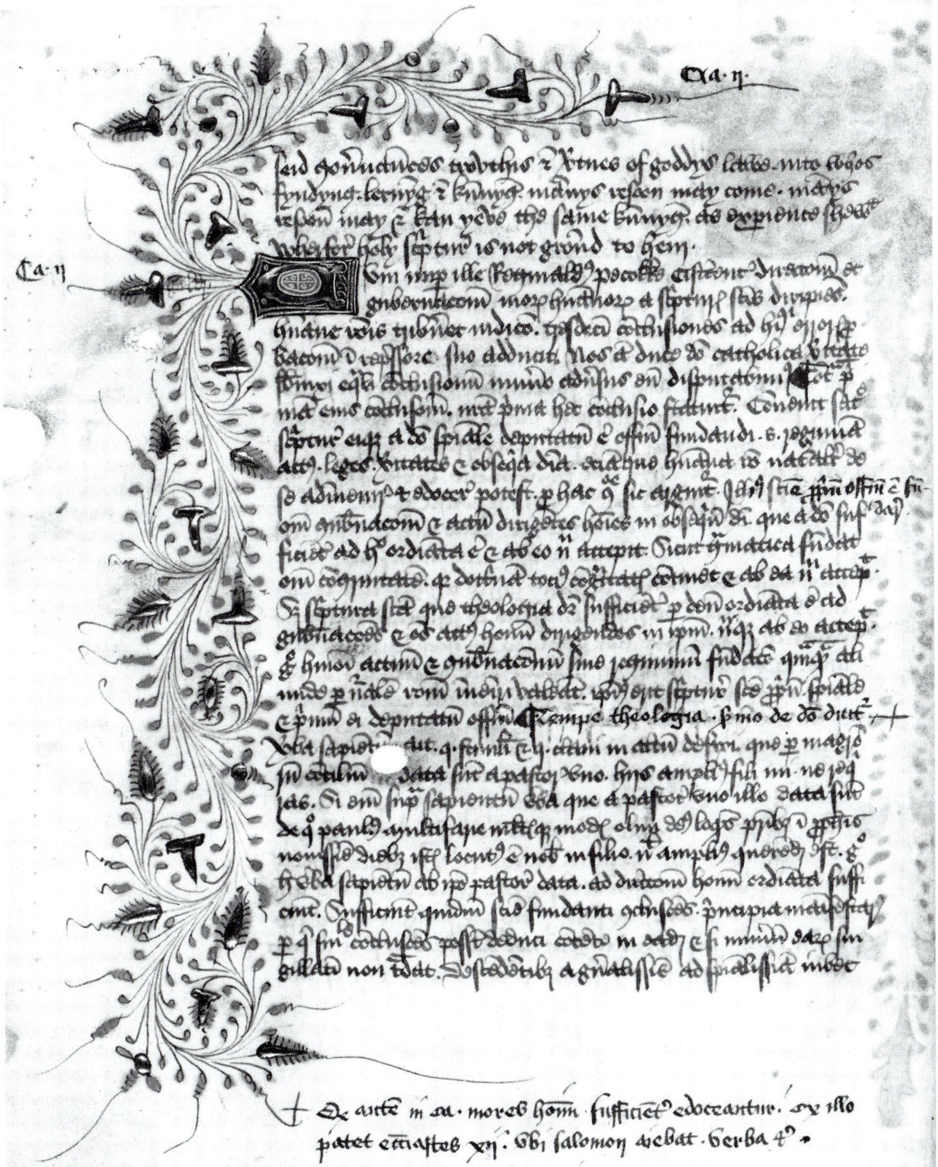

Plate XXVIIb John Bury, *Gladius Salomonis*, text page, champ initial with elongated spray

1467–1469, ?London

Plate XXVIII

Oxford, Bodleian Library, MS. e
Musaeo 42 (S.C. 3646). Chronicle of the
Kings of England from Adam to Edward
IV, inc. 'Consideryng the lenght and the
hardnesse of holy scripture'.

Datable: after 1467 and before 1469
(based on births of children of Edward IV
mentioned in the MS), prob. London.

Description: parchment; (roll-codex) ii +
35 ff.; 33.6 × 21.2 cm. Lines of descent
in red and green, with main line in dark
rose, gold, and blue; roundels in square
frames of rose and green; roundels in
rose and blue surmounted by a gold
crown. 2-line gold and blue letters with
blue and red flourishing; one 4-line gold
letter on rose/blue ground (Pl. XXVIII).
Diagrams. One border, one historiated
roundel (the Fall), f. 1r.

Border: f. 1r. This border takes its beginning from an eight-line initial C
whose letter is in rose and blue on a gold
background, infilled with an aroid and
three pairs of leaves in shaded blue,
rose, and green. The rounded spadix of
the aroid flower is, conventionally, in
orange with yellow dots, and, following
a design of an earlier date (Pls XXIIIa,
XXIV, XXV), crosses diagonally over
the initial space (see Detail). The sprays
are only on two sides of the text space,

88

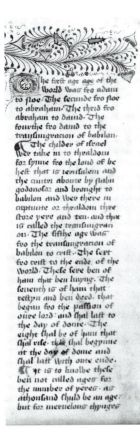

Detail: spiky trefoil, pine cone, and hat flower

at top and L., both positions following general English shop practice for chronicle rolls; only a few have the border extend into the R. margin (cf. Pl. XXII). This artist's style and borderwork, known in other chronicle rolls and other manuscripts, suggest that he was located in London.

The feathering in this border is characterized by penwork in black ink with lines closely applied, forming a heavier central vine than usual. The motifs in pigments are heart-shaped leaves, single leaves, hat flowers (see arrow above initial), and aroids with a flattened or rounded centre, three leaves as calyx, and a gold ball between two sepals or leaves. The L. spray contains an aroid

flower with a more upright centre and a circular base, a less common type of this motif (see arrow in L. margin). The gold motifs in the border are pine cones, engrailed trefoils, and one clasp motif (upper R. spray). The customary gold ball with three green lobes is also present. A branch beside the initial with leaves in colours, more or less curled back on themselves and ending in a stem, is common at this period (see Detail).

Apart from the dense black penwork of the feathering, the overall impression is of a conventional border, almost certainly made by an artist trained in London. His work is known in at least thirteen other manuscripts (Scott, *Survey*).

Plate XXVIII Chronicle of the Kings of England, two-sided spraywork border

London, St Paul's Cathedral, Archive of the College of Minor Canons, deposited at Guildhall, London, as MS. 29413. Letters patent of Edward IV, confirming the charter of Richard II, etc., to the Minor Canons.

Dated: 2 August 1468, wr. Westminster, by Dauysoun.

Description: parchment; 79.3 × 54.7 cm. [measured through glass; without the turn-up]. Calligraphic letters with strapwork ascenders and a radiance. One border, one historiated initial (coat of arms and supporters).

Border: L. margin. The border of this document is truncated at the top because the scribe-calligrapher wrote his text and got in first with tall (5.1–5.2 cm) ascenders that consumed the area normally used for a border (cf. Pl. XXXIV). The other usual border areas, above and to the L. of the initial, were also replaced, in this case, with heraldic motifs: a coat of arms, supporters, badges of the giver, and a standard.

The infilling of the initial contains the arms of England and France supported by a lion and bull, with an inscribed scroll below. Above and outside two angels in gold gowns kneel, holding a royal crown, which is in turn surmounted by a badge used by Edward IV, a double rose (in silver) within a gold radiance. To the L., a white hart ducally engorged and chained stands on a grassy mound and supports a standard with the arms of Edward the Confessor. The angels are rendered in the style of the Abingdon Missal Master, as is the border work (Scott, *Survey*).

The border commences downwards from the grassy mound, with traditional English feathering and mostly English motifs. The curled and open single leaves have long been in the English repertoire but the English trumpet flowers, with six petals and stamen, are somewhat unusual in being shown from behind and barbed. The elliptical motif and the coloured (rose or blue) triangles edged by three gold balls (see R. of initial) are, however, probably foreign in origin, and possibly introduced by the artist of Pl. XXVI. The gold balls near the initial have red colouring on the lobes, probably an early instance of this colouring in place of the standard green. The other gold motifs, balls with three lobes, spiky pine cones, and clasps, are conventional by this time. The feathering is filled out with pen squiggles, especially along the L. edge of the border, the apparent object of the limner being to create a dense decoration, perhaps in response to current fashion and/or the weight of the heraldic ornaments above.

This border represents superior English work near the end of the third quarter of the century and shows as yet little sign of the enlargement of motifs (cf. Pl. XXXVIIa) or a lessening in the quality of drawing motifs (cf. Pl. XXXVIIIb). The artist was previously thought to be from the Oxford area (as in Bodl. MS Digby 227; Scott, *Survey*), but this document brings London forward as an equally good possibility.

Plate XXIX Letters patent of Edward IV, one-sided spraywork border

Plate XXX Charter of Incorporation of the Pewterers' Company, two-sided spraywork border

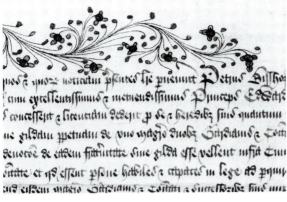

ins̃ a mor̃ uotuatin p̃sntes ls̃e pueuur Petiu Buſſho
aui eyteſſeuntſſumuſ a meweuſuſſumuſ Punceps Eoẽate
S couceſſerr a hreuerdin Beceyr p Se a herebz ſuuſ qudutuuu
uc yilaidiu ppetudiu Se uuo wydeyo Buobz Oiliaiduſ a Coit
Seuoree Se etteui ſurruttte ſuie ilaid eſſe uaſſeut ufid Cuu
uttte et qy eſſeut pſoue hawbileſ a ctpatreſ iu lege aid pquip
aiid euſeui widno Oiuiaiuſ a Coittui a Sucreſſozibz ſuiſ uuu

1473/4,
?London or Westminster

Plate XXX

London, Guildhall Library, belonging
to Pewterers' Company of London, MS
8695. Charter of Incorporation of the
Company by Peter Bishop, William
Large, and Thomas Langtofte.

Date: 1 February 1473/4, probably
London or Westminster.

Description: parchment; 1 membr.; 57.4
× 33.8 cm. (without turn-up). One large,
slightly decorated capital. One border.

Border: top and L. of document. This
border is very unusual for its period
in having no painted motifs and only
a limited selection of gold forms. The
border begins from a 5-line gold letter
(U) on a quartered rose/blue ground
with white filigreework; it is infilled
with a branch of white barbed quatrefoils drawn from upper R. to lower L.
across the interior space. Reservework
flowers are not commonly found with a
champ initial, but are probably indicative of more attention generally being
paid to designs within gold letters. The
split lower stem of the U is also indicative of a later 15th-century style of let-
tering, as seen in full sway in BL Arun-

del 66. The spraywork emerges directly
into two margins (without any interme-
diary motifs such as an acanthus leaf or
aroid flower) as black feathering which
continues across and down the page in a
gently undulating main line with short
branches of feathering to support the
gold motifs. The lobes of the feathering
are nearly rounded and tinted chartreuse
rather than a true green; this colouring
is probably a preference of the limner
rather than a sign of the period. The
gold motifs consist of trefoils, a spiky
pine cone, and, mainly, balls with three
lobes tinted in rose. The rose tint is another unusual trait, and confirmation of
a trend away from green lobes on gold
balls. Certain East Anglian manuscripts
of the 1460s contain borders with only
gold motifs (BL, Cotton MS Vespasian
B.xii; Bodl. MS Bodley 108, q.v., and
Bodl. MS Rawl. liturg. e. 42); the
present border is however unlikely to
have been made in that area of England.

The script is a good version of 'the
common-law hand, less expensive presumably than the chancery style of the
royal charters' (*ex info.* A. I. Doyle),
and the border may be a deliberately
selected, less costly type chosen by the
patrons; it is less expensive for the obvious reason that there is no work in pigments beyond the ground of the initial.

Glasgow, University Library, MS Hunter 77 (T.3.15). Nicholas Love, *Mirror of the Blessed Life of Jesus Christ*.

Date: 1475; wr. by Stephen Dodesham, Sheen Charterhouse: f. iii verso, '. . . the yer of Kynge Edwarde the iiij^the xiij^the.'

Description: parchment; 165 ff.; 28.4 × 20.9 cm. Red underlining. Capitals tinted yellow; red and blue paraffs flourished in red and brown. 2-line blue letters with red flourishing; 3-line coloured letters on gold ground with sprays. One 3-sided spray border, f. 1r; one bar border, f. 3v.

Border: f. 1r. The borders in this manuscript accompany a text that was certainly written in a religious house, but there is no certainty that the decoration was made by a limner resident in the house. In the lightness of its spraywork and the restrained use of acanthus at corners and R. mid-point, the full border (Pl. XXXIb) more resembles a border of 1442 (Pl. XVI), and the style may therefore be an indication of the period in which the limner was trained. The motifs moreover show no familiarity with naturalistic flora and fauna, the new developments in English borders as in the next border, also of 1475 (Pl. XXXII). Ruling for the borderwork is still visible.

Two pages are reproduced in order to show a second type of border hierarchy in a manuscript with only two borders (see also Pls. IIIa–b). If the first border, as opposite at the Table of Contents (f. 1r), is ornamented with a lesser design, the second border at the first text page will normally have a full border with sprays on all four sides. No rigid rules, however, apply to English manuscripts: some instances are also known of a full border at the index and a partial border at the first page.

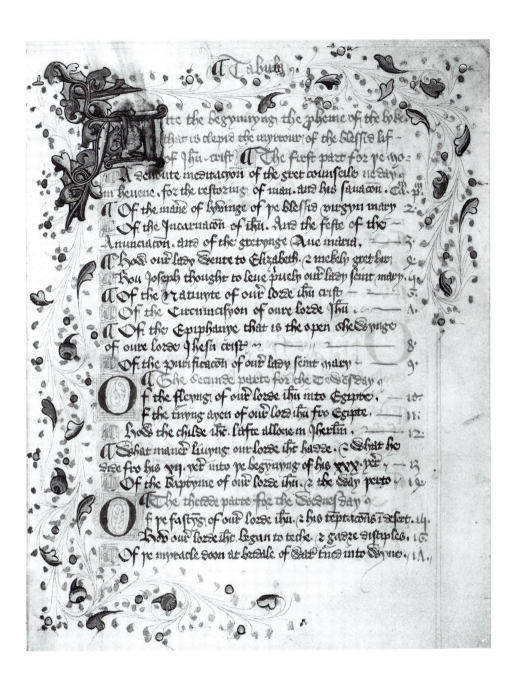

f. 3v. The full border in this manuscript is made up of a standard English bar-frame, with pink and blue acanthus scrolled over and under three bars replacing mid-points normally punctuated with acanthus or a large aroid. The spray penwork develops from a corner, from the stub of a vine on the bar-frame, or from the lobes on a leaf. Another unusual characteristic is the presence of brief sprays between the columns, apparently a random occurrence during the century (cf. Pl. IV) instead of a bar (Pls II, VI, XVI). The coloured motifs (barbed quatrefoils, kidneys, and trumpets) are standard in design, apart from cup flowers at upper L. and lower R (see arrow). At this late period it is rare to see barbed quatrefoils (see arrow), which are more common in the first 20–30 years of the century. The initial contains two aroids that are of a small size and style also more familiar in the second quarter of the century.

The colours are, as commonly, pink, rose, blue and green, with a few motifs in murky orange. The penwork of the feathering is in a brown ink, which gives an impression of airyness (cf. Pls XVI, XXV), especially in contrast to motifs outlined in black.

All in all, the style of the two borders would *appear* to date from the later second quarter, and this instance is a cautionary tale with respect to the period of training of the artist and the actual date of a manuscript.

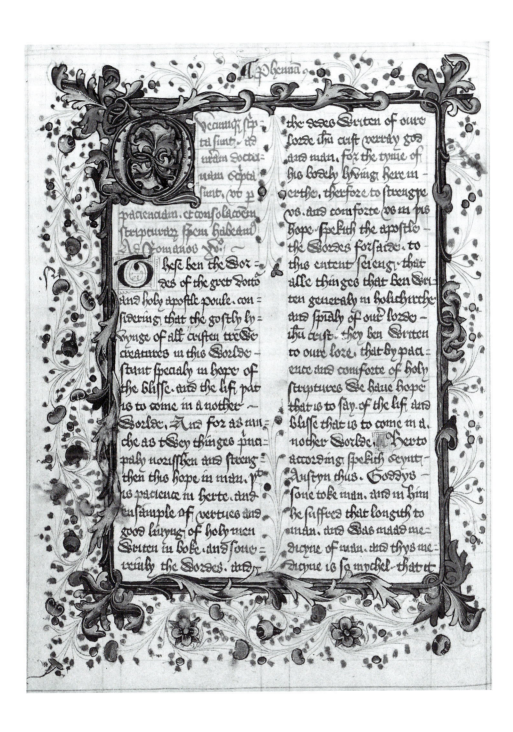

Plate XXXIb Nicholas Love, *Mirror of the Blessed Life of Jesus Christ*,
first text page, full bar border

97

Luton, Art Museum. Luton Guild Register (ff. 1r–6v, Calendar; ff. 7r–12v, blanks). Arms of Archbishop Thomas Rotherham.

Date: 1475 (year of opening list of members).

Description: parchment; 130 ff; 28.6 × 20.5 cm. Text in blue, gold, and red, variously; rose line endings. Calligraphic ascenders. 1-line capitals in rose and blue; 4-line gold letters on a rose/blue ground with sprays. 51 full and partial borders, often historiated, usually with coats of arms; 1 full-page miniature, f. 13v (Crucifix-Trinity).

Border: f. 13r. This border shows a new stage of structural development with respect to integrating the English style of borderwork with continental motifs. That is, it has a fully English introductory initial and a full bar-frame border with, at the corners, large clusters of acanthus and/or fantastic double aroid flowers. The border, however, no longer shows English feathering or motifs in the areas between the corners. Apart from a few gold balls with (uncoloured) pen lobes, the motifs are either naturalistic, i.e. columbines, roses, blue thistles with bracts, strawberries, and carnations (pinks), or they are standard continental introductions, i.e. round ball-like flowers (poppyheads) or apparently realistic blue and red flowers (?forget-me-nots). The fine collared parrot and the squirrel with nut are non-English motifs that by this time are found in other English manuscripts (e.g. Bodl. Hatton 10). Also new are double lines in rose ink framing the border space, another continental introduction. The very large size of the introductory initial (6.7 × 7.5 cm.) relative to the text space (16 × 11.2 cm.) was not common in English manuscripts until this period (the provincial initial in Pl. XIX is an exception).

This border may have been made by two limners, one of English and one of continental training, or by one English artist skilled in both styles. Because of overlap in the use of colour between the initial and the border motifs, the latter option is probably more likely. The colouring is very fresh, and the page is reproduced for its standard colouring and renderings, i.e. for English motifs: the faded rose and brilliant blues of the initial and bar frame and the orange or rust of the aroids; and for continental flowers and leaves, what seems to have been standard usage: two shades of roses, pink and red; blue and deep lavender for columbines; rosey pinks; blue thistles with shaded bracts; red strawberries with yellow dots; and green ciliate leaves. Note the branch of poppyhead flowers in five different colours (L. border).The gold background areas are very unusual at this period for having stippled designs of circles and rows of dots.

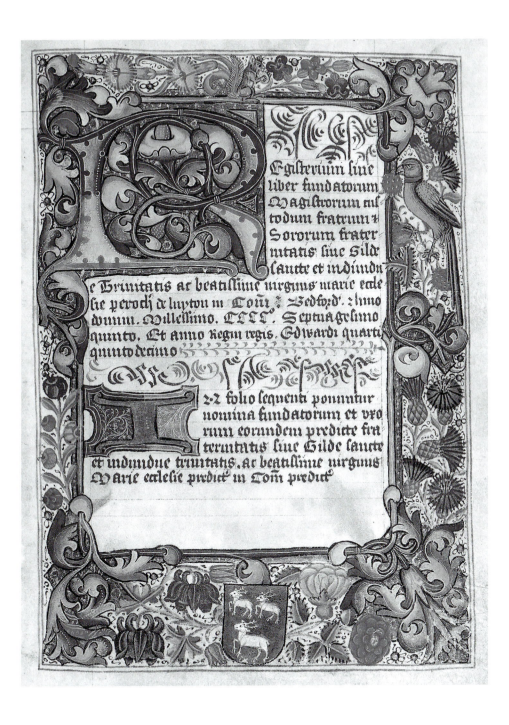

London, belonging to the Skinners' Company. Book of the Fraternity of the Assumption of Our Lady (Lat. and Eng.).

Dated: 17 Edward IV [=1477/8]; prob. London.

Description: parchment; 110 ff.; 41 × 28.3 cm. Line endings. 1-line red and blue letters; 2-, 3-, 4-, and 5-line blue letters with red flourishing from f. 2r; reservework initials from f. 27v. Numerous borders after f. 32v (some with historiated initials, mainly of the Company badge of an ermine cap and crown); three miniatures, ff. 32v, 34v, 41r.

Border: f. 35v. The border here begins from a five-line gold letter on a rose/blue ground bearing white filigreework. This type of border probably derives from either the spray or the champ initial, in which the spraywork was extended to fill two or more sides of the text space.

The limner has been identified as the English artist of the two borders in Bodl. MS Bodley 283 and in a considerable number of other manuscripts (Scott, *Survey*, no. 136), his work being found here for the first time in a dated book. In the L. and lower margins the raceme-like feathering in black ink trails in a gentle wave down the page, bearing shorter vines that curl into a distinct circle to enclose a motif in mixed rose, blue, and gold. These motifs are composed of coloured trefoils or quatrefoils marked with white circles or dots and hedged with gold balls, gold pine cones, or gold trefoils against the edge of the coloured part of the motif. These ornaments were probably originally an import from the continent, though by this time and in in this context are not noticeably foreign. The gold balls with three green lobes and the green-tinted lobes of the feathering are on the other hand entirely English, as are the gold trefoils. The feathering is of course also English. The lobes of the concluding motif in the lower border are tinted rose and blue, a happily datable instance of this practice; the change from green to red or red and blue lobes seems to begin *c.* 1470 (see Pl. XXX).

This border is interesting as a record of the comfortable use of motifs that combine both colours and gold, a not particularly common phenomenon in the conventional English stock. The slightly elongated finials or lobes of the feathering, especially as in the upper margin, bent back towards the black vinework, are a characteristic of this limner. The border is also important for a dating of the motifs mentioned above, as a status-check on the standard English style in the late 1470s, and useful for its firm dating for the limner.

Plate XXXIII Book of the Fraternity of the Assumption of Our Lady,
     spraywork border

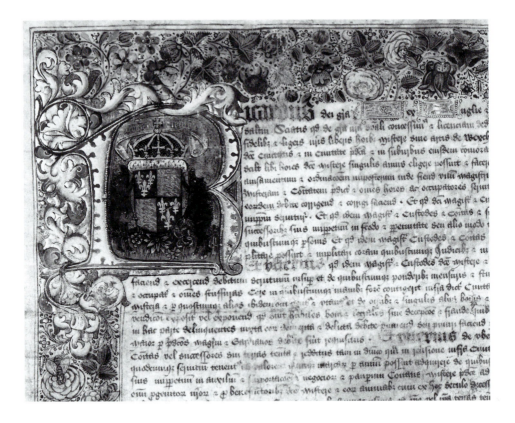

1484, Westminster

Plate XXXIV

London, belonging to the Wax Chandlers' Company. Charter of Incorporation to Company of the Wax Chandlers of London.

Date: 16 February 1484; Westminster, ?wr. by [?John] Gunthorp.

Description: parchment. 1 membr.; 47.5 × 22.7 cm. (without turn-up). Six gold letters with rose or blue flourishing [first line]. One historiated initial (arms and supporters of Richard III).

Border: top, L., & R. of document. This border shows various features of late book decoration in England. There is, above all, a not unusual but still remarkable mix of English and continental designs and motifs. The huge 13-line initial **R** contains the royal arms of England with boar supporters (badge of Richard III) surmounted by a crown with crimson cap and ermine lining, and Richard III's motto on a scroll above. The letter, halved between rose and blue, has typical white shading with dots and circles along the inner edge and wavy fret-work along the outer side. The coloured triangular inset in the initial ground (in the exterior angle of the **R**) is also typical English handling of this area (cf. Pls II, XXXII, XXXVIIIb), if probably a limner's preference rather than a datable practice. English vines and acanthus leaves branch out from two corners of the letter and curl back to form a roundel that encloses a small aroid flower. With these motifs, the

Englishness ends. The rest of the border is entirely continental in style and might even have been done by a second artist.

The theme of the rest is naturalism, with flowers, fruits, and creatures made life-like to the best of the artist's ability. The border in fact teems with animate forms, and every other millimeter of space is filled out with circles, squiggles, pen marks, gold balls with lobes, and coloured triangles with gold balls. The border differs from other mixed-style decoration (Pls XXVI, XXXVb) in that it is packed solid and less connected between major motifs, whereas other borders kept the regularity given to a border design by feathering.

The lower L. margin begins with a branch of three pink roses, two inhabited by a bee (see Detail overleaf), symbol of the Wax Chandlers, to the artist at least. In an innovation indicative of the late date, several leaves and the bee wings are rendered in wash gold. The branch is not connected to the decoration above it. The natural display continues in the upper margin with a branch of flowers, of strawberries, more roses and a bee, a columbine and leaf, a violet with bee, daisies with a bee, a peacock in its splendor, thistles, and more bees, etc., ending in the lower R. with a mixed branch of thistles and carnations, and a bee.

Other continental features are the double rose lines, the fine multi-coloured acanthus branch (R. upper corner), and the lack of a bar frame, with little structural relationship between the English and foreign styles.

Plate XXXIV Charter of Incorporation to Company of the Wax Chandlers,   103
three-sided borders within double pen lines

London, British Library, Additional MS 33736. Pietro Carmeliano of Brescia, *Suasoria laetitiae ad Angliam pro sublatis bellis civilibus et Arthuro principe nato epistola* [*Laus Angliae*].

Datable: *c.* 19 September 1486 (presentation copy to Henry VII, prob. at the birth of his son Arthur); prob. London.

Description: parchment; 14 ff.; 18.9 × 13 cm. In rose: paraffs, titles, running titles. One 2-line gold letter on rose/blue ground. One border, f. 2r; one full-page miniature, f. 1v (coat of arms with angel-supporters and badges).

Border: f. 1v. This double opening was selected partly in order to demonstrate the change in location and importance of coats of arms with respect to borders and partly as evidence of the changing structure of borders. Earlier in the period coats of arms were placed either at the mid-point of a lower border (Pls II, XXIIIa) or within an introductory initial (Pls XII, XVI); in the second half of the century there was a decided tendency to enlarge ownership marks and to use them as an illustration in their own right, as here. These royal arms were turned into a striking frontispiece by surmounting them with a royal crown and providing large angel-supporters with wings brilliantly coloured in red and blue. Badges of the king, a hound couchant and red and white roses, fill in with further allusions to the royal destination. The rose badges are repeated in the border opposite, together with another badge, the red dragon of Wales.

f. 2r. The structure of the border on f. 2r, like that on Pl. XXXIV, is quite different from the conventional English design. There is no bar frame to support the spraywork, which here originates illogically on three sides from a small motif at the centre of the text; even the initial is not attached to spraywork. The rose branches are also independent of other motifs. Like other foreign-influenced borders (Pls XXXII, XXXIV), this border is contained by a double pen outline in pink ink. Certain ideas and aspects of earlier English design do however survive: the rose badges are located at corners where vine, aroid, or acanthus roundels used to stand; and the spraywork in the L., upper, and R. borders begins at a mid-point as if from acanthus clusters on a bar. The badge at the mid-point of the lower border was also the usual place for heraldic items in earlier borders. Other continental elements are (i) lobes on gold balls half coloured (in red or blue) and half in white, in contrast to earlier, fully coloured lobes (in green); and (ii) a new type of initial, very angular in form, with splayed feet and triangular stems, bars, and serifs.

Although the border is not of a fundamentally English design, the maker of these pages was probably an English artist who had his standard motifs (sprays, lobed gold balls, trefoils, pine cones, feathering) cohabit with new ones, managing to keep some indigenous flavour to his border.

Plate XXXVa Pietro Carmeliano, *Suasoria laetitiae ad Angliam*,
frontispiece

Petri Carmeliani Brixiensis poetę Suasoria
Lętiię ad angliam pro sublatis bellis ci
uilibus et Arthuro prīcipe nato epistola

Nglia post tātas clades tātas q̃ ruinas
Et tot cognata pręlia facta manu c
Post odiuȝ antiquum geminę de sanguiē regu
Stirpis et innumeras gentis utriq̃ neces
Te superum rector tandem prospexit ab alto
Cum facies esset tam miseranda tibi
Vndiqȝ ciuili cum sanguine terra maderet
In qȝ tuis populis Luctus ubiqȝ foret
Cum genitrix natum natus fleretq̃ parêteȝ
Et fratrem frater nupta pudica uiruȝ
Filius et patrem fratrem quandoqȝ necaret
Frater et is furens iret in omne nefas

Plate XXXVb Pietro Carmeliano, *Suasoria laetitiae ad Angliam,*
first text page, full border within double lines

1492, London

Plate XXXVI

London, Victoria and Albert Museum, National Library of Art, MS L. 4362-1948. Grant of Arms by John Wrythe, Garter King of Arms, to Hugh Vaughn (Fr.).

Dated: 3 April 1492, London.

Description: parchment; 1 membr.; 49.4 × 29 cm. (without turn-up). Decorated ascenders. One historiated border (coat of arms, mantle, helm, crest, and banner).

Border: top & L. of document. This border returns us to the arena of English illumination, and it is perhaps not surprising to find the office of the Garter King of English arms as a conservative purveyor of English decoration. The L. border contains the arms granted to Hugh Vaughn with the relevant appurtenances, including a helm, dagged mantle, torse, and crest of a young man holding an upturned knife; above, a banner bears a cross and a man with upturned knife swimming through water indicated by wavy lines of blue and rose.

The initial is large (4.9 × 7.2 cm.) and wholly English, with the letter divided between pale rose and blue, having inside and out acanthus leaves in blue, pale rose, green, and orange. One of these leaves is, however, rendered mainly in grey, an innovation in colouring in the last quarter of the century. Some of the smaller motifs in the border are also in grey.

The structure of the border reflects a mainly English design with some continental elements. The L. border begins as

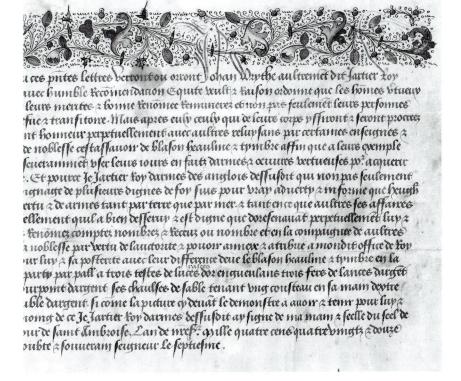

two green stalks below the coat of arms without a rationalized starting point. The work in the upper border is however rationalized by the large acanthus leaf and the vine of feathering that branches to hold trumpet flowers, small veined leaves, and larger single acanthus leaves. The feathering and motifs are English, while the background of pen-and-ink squiggles is continental in style (cf. Pl. XXVI). The gold balls have un-coloured loops rather than tinted lobes, and the petals of the barbed quatrefoils near the initial are made to resemble loops rather than petals, an indication of the late date. The other gold motifs are conventional: clasps, trefoils, and spiky trefoils.

As sometimes customary later in the century, the colours are more muted than, for instance, in the Luton Guild Register (Pl. XXXII; colour pl. p. 19): the greens and blues are dampened, less intense, and the rose colour contains strong ingredients of tan and white. The acanthus leaves within the initial are the only motifs to show mid-century English intensity of colouring.

This border, then, shows yet another means of combining English and continental styles. Here the background and the vine stalks are continental, while the motifs and initial colouring are English. There is no English bar frame (which may occur at this period), nor, on the other hand, are there pink framing lines so often found in borders with continental influence.

The document, in a bastard secretary script, is not by the hand of the Garter King, who signed it as supervising official (*ex info.* A. I. Doyle).

Plate XXXVI Grant of Arms by John Wrythe, two-sided spraywork border   109

London, Public Record Office, E 164/ 11. *Statuta Angliae,* 1 Ed. IV–11 Hen. VII (ff. 1–92v), continued to 7 Hen. VIII (Fr. and Eng.).

Datable: *c.* 1496, prob. London (on grounds of scribe): f. 90v, to 11 Hen. VII (acceded August 1485).

Description: parchment; iii + 196 ff.; 38.5 × 24.7 cm. Running and other titles with red and blue paraphs. 4-line gold letters on rose/blue ground with white designs, with sprays, in pen box. Titles in scrollwork (see pl. opposite). At a first regnal year, full border, with coat of arms, historiated initial (king, enthroned, and courtiers), ff. 3r (Ed. IV), 41r (Rich. III), and 48r (Hen. VII).

Border: f. 41r. This border shows a common loosening of the controlled English borderwork of earlier decades. The most obvious change shows in the motifs of the spraywork. Although the leaf motifs are regularly spaced and balanced against each other, they are much larger and fewer than in earlier borders, even in books of approximately the same size. The shading and cross-hatching are considerably more obtrusive on these motifs and lack the organic shadowing of earlier motifs. The kidney leaf in the upper border is also enlarged; and it is flattened in order to keep to the unspoken outline of the border. This plank-like shape for borders is a characteristic of later English manuscripts and almost certainly owes its straight outline to erased quidelines. The acanthus and aroid motifs in the two lower corners are less enlarged and do not really fit the space normally occupied by corner-pieces. They are identical in colouring and design to the cornerpieces on f. 48r, and it is likely that all were drawn from a standard pattern used for a smaller book. All three borders have royal arms at the mid-point of the lower border. The book is likely to have been produced for Henry VII, for whom the artist illustrated other books.

Another change is the use of vertical white lines for shading of the large initial **R** rather than a fretted white design. An oddity, rather than a change, is the lack of tint of any colour on the feathering.

Plate XXXVIIa *Statuta Angliae*, opening page for reign of Richard III 111

F. 51v. The 4-line initials in this manuscript are interesting in that their sprays are rigidly enclosed in rectangles (outlined in pink) and in that they have unconnected strewn motifs of sprigs of strawberries (e.g. ff. 7r, 11r, 27v, 36v, 51v), poppyhead motifs, and cup flowers (e.g. ff. 17v, 51v, 80r, 83r), and other types of flowers (e.g. ff. 17v, 51v, 80r, 83r). Motifs that are not joined to other motifs in the context of a spray are strange indeed and in need of a pen box to suggest the connection with the initial.

Plate XXXVIIb *Statuta Angliae* (detail, enlarged),
spray initial in pen line

Oxford, Merton College, MS 23. St Jerome, *In duodecim minores prophetas*. For Richard Fitzjames, Warden of Merton, 1483–1507, bp of Rochester, 1497–1503.

Datable: during/shortly after 1497: f. 237v, 'Explicit/liber explanacionis beati Jeronimi . . . in Vigilia Sancti Hugonis Anno/dominice incarnacionis. 1497.'

Description: parchment; 237 ff.; 39 × 25.6 cm. In red: signatures, introductions, running titles, capitals. 3-line blue and red letters with red and brown or black flourishing; 4-, 5-, or 9-line gold letters on rose/blue ground with sprays; 10-line gold letters on gold base with red and blue insets and coat of arms; 8-line coloured letters on gold ground with sprays (Pl. XXXVIIIb). One historiated border (kneeling ecclesiastic), one historiated initial (St Jerome at lectern), f. 2r (arms excised).

F. 2r. This border, not surprising because of its late date and introductory position, lacks any sign of an English origin, and it may indeed be by a foreign artist. There is no bar frame and no rationalized support for the separate floral and leaf motifs. The continental fondness for placing branches of multi-coloured, elongated acanthus at the corners is realized here with, between them, branches of realistic flowers, notably violets at upper R. and roses and carnations in lower border (both cut). A border ground of black pen squiggles and circles is also familiar as a continental trait, as is the rose pen line around the decoration.

Most of the colouring is muted, again a sign of the late date. Red and green in particular are dampened by comparison with mid- and third-quarter work, and the use of grey for the button flowers in the lower R. vertical border, as well as the shell or wash gold (De Hamel, p. 57) rather than burnished gold, are further traits of the period. Outlining and shading are in rose ink, another innovation of the last quarter.

The one item that has a long history in English border design is the kneeling figure of the patron, in this case, Fitzjames. From as early as the 13th century such figures were placed either outside the initial or at a mid-point in the border. His posture is rationalized here by a chunk of earth.

Plate XXXVIIIa St Jerome, *In duodecim minores prophetas*, opening page   115

F. 39v. After f. 2r, the rest of the decorative work in this manuscript is entirely English in style and rendering, with ordinary motifs that show little or no originality from earlier counterparts. The spray here is made up of unlovely leaves, cup flowers, and one rounded aroid next to the initial. The gold balls once again use green for tint on the half-coloured lobes, and gold pine cones are again at each end of the spray. The work lacks spontaneity, because of less competent drawing and less brilliant colouring. The area occupied by the spray is squared off, adding to the lack of liveliness. The letter is however still crisp in rendering, and the infilling has the coherence of similar, earlier initials.

meos + confiderabo mirabilia de le
tua ambulabit in eis + xpm inuen
et indeos atqz hereticos quos ul p̃r
tatores ul impios fcriptura nou
nunc offendae in eis + infirmari
qz tortuere feneat iuxta illud qd
ypmni eft. Hte pofitus e̅ hic i rui
+ in refur retrioue̅ multoꝝ in ifrael
Explicat explanationu̅ in ofee apl'i
beati ieronimu̅ presbiteri liber t
tuiס ad pamuacchiu̅. Incipit pl
fti ieronimi p̃sbiteri ad pamuachiu̅
explanationem iohelis prophete x

OM. IOHEL:
ordo eft duodeci
pha̅ꝛ aput. h
interp̃tes qui n
breuiat ueritati
retinetur. Ill
ftdm̅ ponunt ar
tertiu̅ micheam
quartu̅ iohel · quintu̅ abdiam · fe
tu̅ ionam · feptimu̅ naum · octa
abatuc. Homu̅ fophoniam · decim
geum · Vndecimu̅ zachariam duod
cinu̅ malachiam · Hebrei autem
ofee qui aput uttrofqz pmus eft · Sed
legunt iohel · tertiu̅ amos · quar
abdiam · quintu̅ ionam · fextum n
tu̅ · feptimu̅ naum · octauu̅ abacu
homu̅ fophoniam · decimu̅ aggeu̅
vndecimu̅ zachariam · duodecimu̅
et ultim⁹ eft malachiam · Et quia
nel omes unu⁹ uolumine ppheta

Oxford, Bodleian Library, MS Selden supra 77 (S.C. 3465). William Parron, of Piacenza, *De astrorum vi fatali.* Dedicated to Henry VII.

Datable: wr. by 15 October 1499: f. 55r, prob. London.

Description: parchment; 58 ff.; 16.7 × 12.5 cm. In red: ruling, titles. One blue and gold line-ending, f. 4r (Pl. XXXIX). 1-line blue and gold letters with red and blue flourishing; one 2-line gold letter on a rose/blue base (Pl. XXXIX). One border, one historiated initial (king-and-court scene), f. 4r.

Border: f. 4r. This latest and last style in English borderwork is almost completely removed from the structure and motifs of the first three quarters of the century, and even from many borders of the fourth quarter. The branches of flowers and of acanthus lie on an unadorned base of shell or wash gold. There is no bar frame, as we have already seen in other borders, and no English spraywork as survived in some late manuscripts (Pls XXXVb, XXXVIIa). Each motif lies on the background, unconnected to any other and only related by general genre of plant life. But if the motifs are 'strewn,' they are nevertheless organized. There is still some sense of the importance of corners as witnessed by the formal, elongated acanthus, and two nearly equal flower-sprigs share the vertical space between corners. The acanthus stablizes the border through its repetition in the same colours (rose and blue) and in similar layout. The central positions of the upper and lower margins are occupied by a single sprig or branch (smaller at top, larger with two flowers at bottom) and emphasize, as previously in the century, the importance of this decorative site. The lack of spraywork and/or pen squiggles on the gold background call particular attention to the remaining motifs – that were still at this date of most importance to the border artist.

This type of border, sometimes made by a native artist and sometimes by a continental artist working in England, is not uncommon at the end of the 15th century and in the first quarter of the 16th (cf. Pächt and Alexander, Pl. CVII, nos 1168c, 1170; Pl. CVIII, no. 1171). The type may co-exist in manuscripts with English borders that are traditional in design or with borders that are a mix of English and continental elements. Because of the clearly English hand in the miniature of a king-and-court scene, it is likely that this border was made by an English limner imitating a foreign style. The border can be regarded as the last stylistic development of English border decoration in manuscripts made in the 15th century. Other borders were made in books well into the 16th century but would draw for their designs and motifs on this kind of style, on traditional English border designs, or on the work of known continental artists, such as Gerard Horenbouts of Ghent (Alexander and Temple, Pl. LVII, nos. 827, 828). The artist of this initial also made the historiated initial on Pl. XXXVIIa.

Plate XXXIX William Parron, *De astrorum vi fatali*,
  full border in pen line

119

daisy heads with stem on inside of band frame, 1394–1397

curled leaves with gold spike motif, 1395–1399

trellis band border with columbine, 1394–1397

white bands of shading on leaves, *c.* 1403

filigree band border with corner roundel of vines and leaves, 1406

interlace with sprig, *c.* 1403

circular shading in white on leaves, 1406

trumpet flower, large aroid with white striations, small aroid, spiky gold trefoil, 1445/6

pairs of gold balls with green sqiggles and deeply curled leaves, 1425

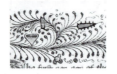

worm-like aroid, 1435

heart motif, gold clasp and gold pine cone, 1467–1469

barbed quatrefoil, 1453–1459

Late fourteenth- and fifteenth-century English motifs (not to scale)

GLOSSARY

Acanthus: a multilobed leaf, often elongated, twisting around itself or a bar (Pls XII, XXXIb); used as: the beginning point of a spray or other decorative work (Pl. XX), cornerpieces (Pl. VIII) and midpoints (Pl. XVIII) of a border, single leaves in spraywork (Pl. XXIIIa), the infilling of an initial (Pl. XXIIIa), and in and around an introductory initial (Pl. XXXII); a very common motif in English 15th-century book decoration.

Aroid: a fantastic or pseudo-flower with a spadix (q.v.) in various possible forms and usually marked as with seeds, enclosed in sepals of a plain or ruffled style; a favourite stylized flower of much of 15th-century border decoration, used in sprays (Pl. XIV), at corners (Pl. XXIIIa), in initials (Pl. XIX), and to introduce sprays (Pl. XXVIIa).

Background: the surface, whether coloured, patterned (Pl. X), of gold (Pl. XXXIX), or void (Pl. XVIII, border), on which a miniature, initial, or parts of a border are laid.

Badge: an animal or object used as the sign of a person or of allegiance to a person; may be shown with arms, worn on clothing, on banner, or applied to an object such as plate, roof bosses, textiles, jewels, and books (Pl. XXXVb, lower margin).

Balls, gold: a very common element of English 15th-century border decoration; appears on the feathering of spraywork (Pl. XIII) or as single motifs around a bar-frame (Pl. XII); often with one to four pen squiggles (Pl. XII), with (Pl. XVIII) or without green or other colour on lobes (Pl. XXXVI); not used within initials and only rarely within miniatures (Pl. XXXV);

combined with coloured triangles, etc., later in the century (Pl. XXXIII).

Band Border: a border composed of a bar and, outside of it, panels in alternating colours decorated with filigreework or monochrome designs (usually acanthus or scrollwork; Pl. VI); sometimes a full border and sometimes combined with a bar-frame on one or more (Pl. VI) sides; usually indicates an important text division.

Bar frame: the part of an English border that lies closest to the text space; composed of a frame of gold and of a vine of alternating lengths of rose and blue, which may show growth of a vine stub or leaf (Pl. XVIII); leaves, other motifs, and spraywork may originate from it at corners and mid-points.

***Champ* initial:** a French term used to refer to a ground in decoration and espoused in English limning shops to refer to gold letter on a rose/blue ground with white designs and usually with a brief spray of feathering and gold motifs (no coloured motifs; Pl. XXVIIb); a description not always rigorously followed by limners (the sprays in Pl. XXVIIb are, for instance longer than normal).

Cinquefoil: *see* **Quatrefoil, barbed.**

Clasp: a small rectangular motif of gold that seems to hold strands of feathering, in the manner of a hair clasp (Pls XXVIII, XXIX).

Column border: a border with a bar-frame between two columns of text and sprays at top and bottom (cf. Pl. XXV); or the part of a full border between two columns of text Pls. I, II, VI).

Cornerpiece: a decorative element, such as an interlace (Pl. ia), grotesque (Pl. ii upper R.), roundel, or cluster of leaves (Pl. xiii) at the right-angle join of two sides of a bar frame.

Curvifoliate: leaves folded back on themselves (Pl. ib, lower border).

Daisy bud: the bud of a daisy seen in profile with green calyx and closed petals in pink and white (Pls ii, L. border; iiia); may be more or less recognizable.

Engrailed: used here for the edges of a ground, usually of gold, whose sides have low, continuous, and joined curvilinear indentations or arcs (cf. Pls xva–b).

Feathering: the basis of much spraywork on English 15th-century borders and initial extensions (cf. Pls xxx, xxxviiib); consists of short pen lines roughly equal in length and equidistant apart, in black or brown ink, whose ends are drawn together to form a central vein or stem with the other end terminating in a small plain rounded or oval lobe or finial, in a curve, or in a squiggle; as a whole, raceme-like in shape (Pl. xxxiii); often supporting gold (cf. Pl. xxx) and/or coloured motifs (cf. Pl. xviii); lobes/finials at first void, later often tinted green, then red or blue, and finally left partly void and partly with colour; used on both partial (cf. Pls xiv, xxia) and full borders (cf. Pls xvi, xxxib).

Filigreework: a delicate design of lines, vines, flowers, etc.; here usually in white on a coloured ground (letter U of Pl. xxx; letter I of Pl. xxxii; letter T of Pl. xxxiii).

Flourishwork border: a border made only of penwork (and possibly some brushwork), usually mainly in red and blue, sometimes with lavender, gold, or green; often an elongated bracket-like design next to the text space, with roundels and pen flourishing at corners; may occur with a two-coloured, parted letter; for only example here, cf. Pl. ib, col. B, with roundels at the initial E and flourishing at the bottom (letter not parted).

Flowers: *see* **Leaves**

Gold: *see* **Balls; Pine cone; Shell; Stippled.**

Grotesque: an animal of a bizarre, unreal nature (Pl. ii, upper R. corner) or composed of parts of one or more real animals (hybrid); sometimes also refers to human figures in borders.

Ground: *see* **Background.**

Gutter: the channel between two pages of an open, bound book.

Hatching/hatchwork: a means of shading or tempering the colour of a motif by a series of parallel lines; in this period, usually in white or yellow;
cross-hatching: crossed lines used for the same purpose (*see* initial S of Pl. xx; or H of Pl. xxiv).

Historiated: refers to a scene (Pls ia, ii, xviia, xxxviia, xxxviiia), figure or part-figure (Pls xvb, xxii), or a coat of arms (Pls xii, xvi, xxvi, xxix), etc., in a border or initial;
historiation: a miniature or figure in an initial or border; not used to refer to a miniature.
See also **Inhabited.**

Inhabited: a border incorporating representational images such as an animal or bird (Pl. xxxii), a human figure (Pl. xxxviiia), a grotesque (Pl. xva), or naturalistic plants (Pls xxxii, xxxvb, xxxix).

Interlace: in borders, an illusionistic design created (usually) by vines in different colours apparently woven over and under each other; used as cornerpieces of a border (Pl. ia, lower R. corner) or at mid-points on a border (Pl. iv), and as components of a letter (cf. Pl. ib), usually in the first two decades of the 15th century and earlier; occasionally revived later in the 15th century (cf. Pl. xviib, mid-point of L. border).

Leaves:
bell (Pl. xviii), **heart** (Pl. xxib), **holly** (Pl. viii, top), **kidney** (Pls xxxib, xxxviia), **kite** (Pl. ii), **trumpet** (Pl. viii), leaves or flowers of a form roughly similar to their name. It is uncertain whether these motifs were meant to be leaves or flowers by medieval limners.

ciliate: leaves fringed at their margins with delicate hairs that are normally rendered in black in English book art (Pl. xxxiv, lower L.; Pl. xxxv). See also **Single leaf; Trefoil**.

Limner: also called 'illuminator' and 'enlumineur'; the term for the craftsperson who made miniatures and/or the borders and initials in pigments and gold in medieval books; not used for a flourisher.

Lobe: a rounded or pointed, projecting part of a leaf with a separation between another lobe or part of the leaf; here also used to indicate rounded or oval additions to gold balls and rounded or oval finials on feathering.

Mask: a formalized, frontal head of an animal; may be nondescript or, as often, a lion's head; may have protruding tongue or be enfolded in leaves (cf. Pl. ii, lower R. corner; Pl. iv, initial).

Motif: an element of decoration.

Monochrome: an adjective used to describe a design or motif made and shaded in a single colour.

Nebuly: a stylized (rather than naturalistic) cloud rendered as a regular pattern of wavy lines, of two or three possible forms.

Nota bene **hand:** a hand, which may be in a cuff, sleeve, or glove, that points to a passage in a text important to the maker/drawer of the hand, whether the scribe following an examplar with such hands, an early owner, or an owner from a later period [none reproduced here].

Parted letter: a letter of the alphabet whose components are separated by a narrow void of bare parchment or paper, usually lengthwise between two colours [none reproduced here].

Pine cone: a gold, pine cone shaped motif with black lines to indicate seed (Pls xxiv, xxviib).

Poppyhead motif: a round, ball-like motif or flower with vertical panels indicated (Pls. xxvi, xxxii); sometimes with opening at top and stamens; may also resemble a rose hip or hawthorne berry; a later 15th-century continental introduction to English borderwork; also called 'balloon' flower (Scott, *Survey*, II, 369).

Quatrefoil, barbed: a four-petalled flower with pointed sepals (q.v.) showing between the petals (Pl. xxia, upper and lower sprays); **cinquefoil:** a five-petalled flower, etc.

Raceme: an arrangement of flowers or leaves on short stalks equal in length and separated equally along a central stalk or axis, whether straight or curving (e.g. Pl. xxv, central column; Pl. xxviib)

Reservework: designs, often leaf and vine, created by blanking or hatching out a background in order to leave images on the remaining ground in ground-colour (cf. Pl. VII, infilling of initial).

Rose: a term of colour used here to encompass shades of pink that grade from light to dark rose or maroon, a true pink (Pl. XVIII: col. pl. p. 18, leaves) or a duller less intense pink (Pl. XXXII: col. pl. p. 19, initial, leaves, flowers); one of the two basic colours (with blue) used in 15th-century English border decoration; often used in self-shades on leaves or other motifs; deliberately used in this handbook in a loose manner to cover different tones created by limners or modern photography; also used here to indicate the flower. [The elongated cornerpiece of acanthus on Pl. XXXIX: col. pl. p. 20, lower R. corner, is a shade of rose, whereas the strawberry and one rose are a true red.]

Roundel: a circular space formed by vines in a border (cf. Pl. XVI, lower L. corner; Pl. XXII) or by a miniature frame (cf. Pls. XXII, XXVIII); often used as the concluding end- or cornerpiece of a bar frame and infilled with an aroid (cf. Pl. XVIIa, bottom; Pl. XXIIIa, bottom) or a leaf motif (cf. Pls VA, XIX, top); may appear as a series of round spaces to form trelliswork (Pl. XXII).

Self-colour: here, a means of colouring a motif partly in a lightened version of its own main pigment-colour in order to give the effect of glare light and/or modelling of the motif.

Sepal: a separate division or leaf of the calyx, i.e. the support of leaves that form the outer covering of a bud or flower above the stem (Pls. XXIIIb, XXVIIa, upper R.; XXVIII, R. of initial).

Shell/wash gold: powdered gold mixed with gum arabic and applied to decoration or a background in a diluted manner so as to be luminous but matt and not reflecting of light; not used widely until later in the 15th century (cf. Pl. XXXIX, ground of border and initial). See De Hamel, p. 57

Single leaf: a leaf that is rendered more or less alone on a vine (Pls IX, XX, XXIb) or on spraywork (Pl. VIII, top); may also make up clusters (Pl. XIII) or roundels (Pl. VI) or rows (Pl. VII).

Spadix: the center or fleshy spike-like infloresence of an aroid flower; in 15th-century English border art may be variously shaped, i.e. rounded (Pls XVI, XIX), worm-like (Pl. XIV), enlarged, pointed (Pl. XXIIIb), and/or enclosed in leaves (Pl. XVIII, initial); often decorated so as to appear to be seeded.

Spray initial: an initial composed of a coloured letter on gold ground infilled with coloured or monochrome leaves and with sprays of feathering and coloured and gold motifs (Pl. XXXVIIIb).

Spraywork: decorative work usually beginning from the corner of an initial (Pl. X) or from the mid-point of a bar frame (Pls XVIIb, XIX); made up of feathering (q.v.) and gold and/or coloured motifs; a very common elaboration of a bar frame or of an initial.

Spraywork border: a border composed of an introductory initial and spraywork, without a bar or bar frame (Pls X, XXIV, XXVIIa, XXVIII).

Sprig: a very brief spray of two or three pen lines or feathering supporting two or three gold (Pl. X, at initial) or coloured motifs (Pl. IIIa, end of bar; Pl. VIII, beside initial); often at L. of a large initial (Pls. X, XVI, XVIII, XIX); may also be on bar frame (Pl. XIII).

Squiggle: a single, brief wavy or curlicue line made by a pen, often on feathering (Pl. IIIa) just above two or three short horizontal stokes with a gold ball (Pl. XXIb, top); may be tinted green; frequently used once, three, or four times as the finishing stroke(s) on a gold ball (cf. Pls IV, XIV); also used as background infilling work to create a dense effect in borders later in the 15th century (Pls XXXII, XXXVI, XXXVIIIa); pen circles often used to the same background effect (Pls XXXVI, XXXVIIb).

Stippling/stippled: designs of dots, rings, etc, made with a hard, pointed tool, possibly a single-dot punch, on a gold ground, vine, or letter (visible on Pl. Ia and col. pl., p. 17); dots not punched through the gold surface but made as a depression in the paper-thin gold and the gesso support; used in the late 14th and early 15th centuries, and occasionally in later borders (cf. Pl. XXXII and col. pl., p. 19, gold bar frame and initial); also sometimes referred to as tooling/tooled or stamped (De Hamel, p. 58).

Striation/striated: here referring to a series of more or less parallel lines, usually in white, on a coloured motif such as an acanthus leaf (cf. Pl. XXXII and col. pl., p. 19, above L. of initial) or aroid flower (cf. Pl. XVIII and col. pl., p. 18, sepals in middle of lower border).

Trefoil: a three-lobed or trifoliate leaf; may be in gold or colours (Pl. XXVIIb, top spray; Pl. XXXVI, upper spray) but usually in gold.

Trellis border: *see* Pl. II.

Trumpet motif: a motif shaped like the end of a trumpet; sometimes with petals and/or stamen at the opening (Pl. VIII, spray on bar with both types of trumpet; Pl. XX, upper spray); sometimes used to initiate a border spray or bar (Pl. VIII, L., at initial).

Turn-up: the lower part of a document folded up, usually two to three inches.

Vine: an element of decoration that acts like a vine in supporting branches, leaves, and flowers but that is usually coloured in alternating lengths of red and blue with white designs rather than in a naturalistic colour; used to initiate border sprays, to form roundels, and bar frames, etc.

CHRONOLOGICAL SPREAD BY DECADE OF
MANUSCRIPTS DESCRIBED

1395–1404:

1395–Sept. 1399   [Trinity Hall 17]

c. 1394–97 (?Norwich) [Bodl. Bodley 316]

1396   [BL Harley 401]

c. 1403   [Eton College 108]

1405–1414:

1405   [BL Harley 2946]

1406 (?Glastonbury)   [Bodl. Laud Lat.4]

1408   [Bodl. Fairfax 2]

1410–13 (?London/Westminster)
     [BL Arundel 38]

1415–1424:

1416 (Westminster)   [ERO D/B 3/13/7]

1421/2 (Westminster)
     [BL Harley Ch. 51.H.6]

1425–1434:

1425 (?Lincoln)   [CUL Gg.4.19]

1425–27 (?London)
     [Glasgow UL Hunter 215]

1429 (Oxford)   [CUL Ff.3.27]

1435–1444:

1435 (Oxford)   [Bodl. Bodley 795]

1439–before 1443/4 (?Oxford)
     [BL Royal 5.F.II]

1442 (?Oxford)   [Balliol College 28]

1440–44 (?King's Lynn)
     [Bodl. Duke Humf.b.1]

1445–1454:

c. 1445/6 (?London)   [PRO E 164/10]

1448–55 (?Salisbury)   [Bodl. Bodley 362]

1450 (?London)   [CUL Ee.5.21]

1453–59 (?Salisbury)   [Bodl. Bodley 361]

c. 1453 (?Eastern England)
     [Winchester College 13B]

1454 (Oxford)   [Exeter College 62]

1455–1464:

1456; 1455   [Bodl. Lat.theol.b.5]

c. 1455 (pr. bk.)   [Lambeth Palace 15]

1461   [Balliol College 204]

c. 1457–*c.* 1461 (?Suffolk)
     [Bodl. Bodley 108]

1465–1474:

1467–69 (?London)   [Bodl. e Mus. 42]

1468 (Westminster) [Guildhall MS 29413]

1473/4 (prob. London/Westminster)
     [Guildhall MS 8695]

1475–1484:

1474/5 (Sheen)   [Glasgow UL Hunter 77]

1475 (Luton or London)
     [Luton Art Museum]

1477/8 (prob. London)
     [London, Skinners' Company]

1484 (Westminster)
     [London, Wax Chandlers' Company]

1485–1494:

c. 1486 (prob. London)   [BL Add. 33736]

1492 (London)
     [V & A Nat'l Lib. of Art, 4362-1948]

1495–1499:

c. 1496 (?London)   [PRO E 164/11]

1497   [Merton College 23]

1499–1500 (?London)
     [Bodl. Seld.supra 77]

INDEX OF
OTHER MANUSCRIPTS CITED

INDEX
OF SCRIBES

INDEX OF LOCATIONS /
ORIGINS OF SCRIBES

*The names with an asterisk may have been clerks or supervising officials at a higher level than a scribe, with their signatures being therefore an authorising countersignature to a scribe's work. I am grateful to A. I. Doyle for this information.

BIBLIOGRAPHY

Only a few standard or recent works are listed here for the manuscript entries in the catalogue above. Those works that contain references to more than one catalogue entry are listed first below, followed by an abbreviation that is used in both catalogue entries and in the individual notes to plates below. Further literature concerning the entries may be noticed under notes to plates, p. 130.

Alexander, J. J. G., and E. Temple, *Illuminated Manuscripts in Oxford College Libraries, The University Archives and the Taylor Institution*, Oxford, 1985. [Alexander and Temple]

Bodleian Library, Oxford, *Duke Humfrey's Library & the Divinity School 1488–1988*, exhibition catalogue, 1988. [*Duke Humfrey's Library*]

——, *Summary Catalogue*. [*S.C.*]

Danbury, E., 'The Decoration and Illumination of Royal Charters in England, 1250–1509: An Introduction', in M. Jones and M. Vale, eds., *England and Her Neighbours 1066–1453; Essays in Honour of Pierre Chaplais*, London and Ronceverte, 1989, pp. 157–79. [Danbury]

De Hamel, C., *Scribes and Illuminators* (Medieval Craftsmen Series) London and Toronto, 1992. [De Hamel]

Ker, N. R., *Medieval Libraries of Great Britain: A List of Surviving Books*, 2nd ed., London, 1964. [Ker, *MLGB*]

——, *Medieval Manuscripts in British Libraries*, I: London, Oxford, 1969; II: Abbotsford–Keele, Oxford, 1977. [Ker, *MMBL*]

Ker, N. R., and A. J. Piper, ibid, IV: Paisley–York, Oxford, 1992 [Ker and Piper, *MMBL*]

Pächt, O., and J. J. G. Alexander, *Illuminated Manuscripts in the Bodleian Library Oxford*, Vol. III: British, Irish, and Icelandic Schools, Oxford, 1973. [Pächt and Alexander, III]

Robinson, P. R., *Catalogue of Dated and Datable Manuscripts c. 737–1600 in Cambridge Libraries*, Cambridge, 1988, 2 vols. [Robinson, *Cambridge Libraries*]

Sandler, L. F., *Gothic Manuscripts 1285–1385*, Vol. V of *A Survey of Manuscripts Illuminated in the British Isles*, gen. ed. J. J. G. Alexander, I: Text and Illustrations, II: Catalogue, Oxford, 1986. [Sandler, *Survey*]

Scott, K. L., *Later Gothic Manuscripts 1390–1490*, Vol. VI of *A Survey of Manuscripts Illuminated in the British Isles*, gen. ed. J. J. G. Alexander, I: Text and Illustrations, II: Catalogue, London, 1996. [Scott, *Survey*]

Valentine, Lucia N., *Ornament in Medieval Manuscripts: A Glossary*, London, 1965. [Valentine, *Ornament*]

Watson, A. G., *Catalogue of Dated and Datable Manuscripts c. 700–1600 in The Department of Manuscripts The British Library*, Vol. I: The Text; Vol. II: The Plates, London, 1979. [Watson, *British Library*]

——, *Catalogue of Dated and Datable Manuscripts c. 435–1600 in Oxford Libraries*, Vol. I: The Text; Vol. II: The Plates, Oxford, 1984. [Watson, *Oxford Libraries*]

BIBLIOGRAPHICAL REFERENCES

Plate I: Gordon, Dillian, with C. M. Barron, A. Roy, and M. Wyld, *Making and Meaning: The Wilton Diptych*, National Gallery, London, 1993, pl. 11 (col.) of f. 1r.
Robinson, *Cambridge Libraries*, I: no. 394, II: pl. 178.

Plate II: Ker, *MLGB*, 152.
Pächt and Alexander, III, no. 674, pl. LXX.
Scott, *Survey*, II, 35.
Watson, *Oxford Libraries*, I: no. 77, II: pl. 234.

Plate III: Watson, *British Library*, I: no. 633, II: pl.295.

Plate IV: Ker, *MLGB*, 55.
Ker, *MMBL*, II, 721-2.

Plate V: Watson, *British Library*, I: no. 717, II: pl.312.

Plate VI: Ker, *MLGB*, 91.
Pächt and Alexander, III, no. 797.
Watson, *Oxford Libraries*, I: no. 581, II: pl. 254a, b.

Plate VII: Pächt and Alexander, III, no. 798.
Watson, *Oxford Libraries*, I: no. 485, II: pl. 258.

Plate VIII: Scott, *Survey*, II: no. 50, I: ills. 201-2
Watson, *British Library*, I: no. 433, II: pl. 329.

Plate XI: Robinson, *Cambridge Libraries*, I: no. 43, II: pl. 212.

Plate XII: G. A. J. Hodgett, ed., *The Cartulary of Holy Trinity, Aldgate*, with a note on the illuminations by F. Wormald, London, 1971.
N. Thorp, *The Glory of the Page: Medieval and Renaissance Illuminated Manuscripts from Glasgow University Library*, exhibition catalogue, London, 1987, no. 32, 2 pls.

Plate XIII: Robinson, *Cambridge Libraries* I: no. 32, II: pl. 215.

Plate XIV: Pächt and Alexander, III, no. 898.
Watson, *Oxford Libraries*, I: no. 114, I: pl. 358.

Plate XV: *Duke Humfrey's Library*, no. 32, pl.
Ker, *MLGB*, 143.

Plate XVI: Alexander and Temple, no. 443.
R. A. B. Mynors, *Catalogue of the Manuscripts of Balliol College, Oxford*, Oxford, 1963, pp. xxvi, 20.
Watson, *Oxford Libraries*, I: no. 723, II: pl. 412.

Plate XVII: *Duke Humfrey's Library*, no. 31, pl.
Ker, *MLGB*, 143.
P. J. Lucas, 'An Author as Copyist of his own Work: John Capgrave OSA (1393-1464)', in *New Science Out of Old Books: Studies in Manuscripts and Early Printed Books in Honour of A. I. Doyle*, ed. R. Beadle and A. J. Piper, Aldershot, 1995, pp. 230, 231.
Pächt and Alexander, III, no. 902, pl. LXXXVI.

Plate XVIII: Ker, *MMBL*, I, 190.

Plate XIX: *Duke Humfrey's Library*, no. 46, pl.
Ker, *MLGB*, 143.
Pächt and Alexander, III, no. 1049, pl. XCVII.
Watson, *Oxford Libraries*, I, no. 81.

Plate XX: Robinson, *Cambridge Libraries,* I: no. 26, II: pl. 256.

Plate XXI: *Duke Humfrey's Library*, no. 47, pl.
Pächt and Alexander, III, no. 1053, pl. XCVIII.
Watson, *Oxford Libraries*, I: no. 80.

Plate XXII: Ker and Piper, *MMBL*, IV, 611.

Plate XXIII: Alexander and Temple, no. 586, pl. XXXIV.
Watson, *Oxford Libraries*, I: no. 791.

Plate XXIV: Pächt and Alexander, III, no. 1056, pl. XCVIII.
Watson, *Oxford Libraries*, I: no. 566, II: pl. 531.

Plate XXV: E. König, 'A Leaf from a Gutenberg Bible illuminated in England', *British Library Journal*, 9 (1983), 32–50, esp. 36, 38, 39, 40, 43, figs. 3, 9.

Plate XXVI: Alexander and Temple, no. 579, pl. XXXIII.
Watson, *Oxford Libraries*, I: no. 743.

Plate XXVII: C. Babington, ed., *The Repressor of Over Much Blaming of the Clergy by Reginald Pecock*, Rolls Series 19, London, 1860, Vol. I, p.xl, Vol. II, pp. 567–613, colour frontispiece.
Pächt and Alexander, III, no. 1057.
Scott, *Survey*, II, 308.
R. Sharpe, *A Handlist of the Latin Writers of Great Britain and Ireland before 1540*, Brepols (Belgium), 1997, no. 628, p. 222.

Plate XXVIII: Pächt and Alexander, III, no. 1070, pl. XCIX
Scott, *Survey*, II, 316, 319.
Watson, *Oxford Libraries*, I: no. 654, II: pl. 653.

Plate XXIX: Scott, *Survey*, II, no. 101a (Bodleian MS. Digby 227).

Plate XXXI: A. I. Doyle, 'Stephen Dodesham of Witham and Sheen', in *Of the Making of Books; Medieval Manuscripts, their Scribes and Readers: Essays presented to M.B. Parkes*, ed. P. R. Robinson and R. Zim, Aldershot, 1997, pp. 94–115, esp. pp. 96, 102, 115.
Ker, *MLGB*, 178.
N. Thorp, *The Glory of the Page: Medieval and Renaissance Illuminated Manuscripts from Glasgow University Library*, London, 1987, no. 42, pl.

Plate XXXII: See Pl. XIV, p. 54.
Marks, R., 'Two Illuminated Guild Registers from Bedfordshire', in *Illuminating the Book; Makers and Interpreters: Essays in honour of Janet Backhouse*, ed. M. P. Brown and S. McKendrick, British Library, London, 1998, pp. 120–41.
K. L. Scott, 'The Illustration and Decoration of the Register of the Fraternity of The Holy Trinity at Luton Church, 1475–1546', in *The English Medieval Book: Studies in Memory of Jeremy Griffiths*, ed. A. S. G. Edwards, V. Gillespie and R. Hanna, British Library, London, 2000, pp. 155-183.
Scott, *Survey*, II, pp. 343, 344.
Sotheby's, *Catalogue of the Bute Collection of forty-two illuminated Manuscripts and Miniatures*, 13 June 1983, item 19, frontispiece and six plates.

Plate XXXIII: Scott, *Survey*, II: 328, 330, I: ills. 473–4.

Plate XXXIV: Scott, *Survey*, II, 330.
for John Gunthorpe, see C. E. Wright, *Fontes Harleiani: A Study of the Sources of the Harleian Collection of Manuscripts Preserved in the Department of Manuscripts in the British Museum*, London, 1972, p. 174.

Plate XXXV: Scott, *Survey*, II, 328, 330.
Watson, *British Library*, I: no. 361, II: pl. 846.

Plate XXXVII: Ker, *MMBL*, I, 190–1.
Scott, *Survey*, II, 347.

Plate XXXVIII: Alexander and Temple, no. 618, pl. XXXVI.
Watson, *Oxford Libraries*, I: no. 835, II: pl. 797.

Plate XXXIX: C. A. J. Armstrong, 'An Italian Astrologer at the Court of Henry VII', in *Italian Renaissance Studies: A Tribute to the late Cecilia M. Ady*, ed. E. F. Jacob (London, 1960), pp. 432–54, esp. p. 437.
Pächt and Alexander, III, no. 1125, pl. CVI.
Scott, *Survey*, II, 347, 365.
Watson, *Oxford Libraries*, I: no. 701, II: pl. 803.